Please
Learni
The N
Ext. 24

C000152579

What Do High Performance Managers Really Do?

What Do High Performance Managers Really Do?

PHIL HODGSON
& STUART CRAINER

FINANCIAL TIMES

PITMAN PUBLISHING

Pitman Publishing
128 Long Acre, London WC2E 9AN

A Division of Longman Group UK Limited

© Phil Hodgson and Stuart Crainer, 1993

First published in Great Britain 1993

British Library Cataloguing in Publication Data
A CIP catalogue record for this book can be obtained from the British Library.

ISBN 0 273 60387 6

All rights reserved; no part of this publication may be reproduced, stored
in a retrieval system, or transmitted in any form or by any means, electronic,
mechanical, photocopying, recording, or otherwise without either the prior
written permission of the Publishers or a licence permitting restricted copying
in the United Kingdom issued by the Copyright Licensing Agency Ltd,
90 Tottenham Court Road, London W1P 9HE. This book may not be lent,
resold, hired out or otherwise disposed of by way of trade in any form
of binding or cover other than that in which it is published, without the
prior consent of the Publishers.

Phototypeset in Linotron Times Roman
by Northern Phototypesetting Co. Ltd., Bolton
Printed and bound in Great Britain
by Biddles Ltd, Guildford and King's Lynn

Ashridge is a charity number 311096 registered as Ashridge (Bonar Law Memorial) Trust

'The place where you stand, how you use your space, is the number one priority. How you stand in relation to other people, how you dance with them – that's what it's all about.'
Sean Connery, actor

CONTENTS

INTRODUCTION

Managers appear set on a never ending quest to manage themselves and their organisations more effectively. Bookshelves sag under the weight of insight. New research continually unearths alternative routes to success. Buzzwords enter the increasingly tortuous language of management and, after a short-lived period of popularity, disappear to gather dust.

The relentless process of education and re-definition is, on the surface at least, commendable. Managers want to know more. They are desperate to understand the mechanics of their occupation and how they can enhance their own performance. Unfortunately, they are continually disappointed. Books, magazines, training courses and speeches fall into the trap of the quick fix. Old ideas are re-packaged, highly impressive new terminology is added, and then the market is attacked with gusto. Gurus abound; solutions are a little more scarce.

Too often what is produced is generic. The individual manager has to wade through entire tomes to find sections, sometimes paragraphs, which are appropriate to their own situation. There are nuggets of helpful hints, not the mines of managerial gold they anticipated. For them the search goes on. Libraries become larger, but they are burdened by exhaustive case studies of corporate performance and behaviour. Readers discover how managers in one organisation have been financially successful. The message is usually up-beat – 'You too can have such success,' they say.

Weighty and intimidating, such publications are the coping stone of conventional management education. Case studies undoubtedly help aspiring – and experienced – managers to understand *some* aspects of how companies work. But, the concentration on case studies tends to ignore or gloss over the role of individuals.

Some of the seminal management texts of the last few years have conspicuously failed to bring human relations as a discipline, and individuals as managers, to the centre stage they certainly demand. Michael Porter's *Competitive Advantage*, an academic and bestselling masterpiece of its genre, crams human relations into a couple of paragraphs – the book is over 500 pages long.

On the surface at least this preoccupation was laid to rest in the 1980s. The decade of enterprise and entrepreneurism appeared to place the individual on a pedestal. Leading managers became part of the twentieth-century cult of personality, appearing on chat shows and imparting wisdom. While managers were fêted and put pen to paper to record their secrets for posterity, management theorists discovered quality and excellence.

Yet, even the gurus of quality, excellence and the like tended to sublimate the role of individual managers. They championed (and continue to do so) companies which are 'people-based', but concentrate on team-working and generating group awareness. In his book, *Rebirth of the Corporation*, D Quinn Mills observes: 'Self-managing work teams utilise hierarchical ways of thinking. For example, both hierarchies and self-managing teams speak of reporting relationships and where responsibility is placed.'[1] The old hierarchies live on.

More generally, success and failure are still talked of in corporate terms. The message that people are important is clouded by the preoccupation with corporate performance.

The 1990s has brought its own variations on age-old managerial themes. Corporate re-engineering has emerged as the newest answer to organisational woes. But, its mechanistic interpretation of total quality rests uncomfortably with thoughts of individual development and achievement.

These approaches fail to realise that stories about corporate performance do not explain the successes and failures of individual managers.

THE HOLY GRAIL AND HALLUCINOGENICS

A key contributory factor to this concentration on organisational values and performance has been management's all-consuming love affair with strategy. In the 1960s the world discovered Jimi Hendrix, hallucinogenics and love. Managers discovered strategy. Strategy has developed from a tentative sub-species into the Holy Grail of management theory. Today, it is all embracing. Job titles attract the word 'strategic' as surely as magnets attract steel; business school courses are dominated by the word; enthusiastic business people coo over intricately presented strategic plans.

At its worst, strategy has become pure theory, a means of instilling ascetic logic into the illogical world of business. This approach has succeeded in distancing many of those within organisations from the reality of corporate performance. Strategy – signed, sealed, but not necessarily delivered – has exacerbated the great divide between those who manage and those who sell, produce and service. It has confirmed management's precious status and consigned individuals to the margins.

Managerial faith in the ability of strategy to provide solutions is perhaps another sign of a fundamental lack of confidence in management as a 'profession'. Through their quest for knowledge, for ways of managing better, managers seem sometimes to be seeking to legitimise their own existence. There is – and has been – a fair amount of self-justification in the making of corporate strategy. Strategy has become, for some, the managerial *raison d'être*: I create strategy, therefore I am a manager.

Despite the narrowness of its focus in many businesses, strategy clearly has a crucial place in sound management practice. It cannot be dismissed. Instead, it needs to be utilised to its full potential.

Strategy can be the driving force for corporate change and success. To do so it must address the central problem of turning ideas into action. In many companies this problem has traditionally been ignored – strategy existed; action followed; QED.

In the 1990s, where speed and flexibility are paramount, such assumptions amount to commercial suicide.

LEAVING THE PACK

Akin to the fixation with organisations, this fascination with strategy often negates the roles of individuals. It becomes a process rather than a creative means of enhancing corporate and individual performance. In the mass of data and paper it is easy for the individual manager to be swept along the carefully constructed confines of strategic thought.

This book is a departure from the fascination with all things corporate. It concentrates on the individual within the corporation and corporate strategy, rather than managers as corporate super heroes. It presents practical means for individual managers to improve their understanding of how they manage and, ultimately, their performance.

Robert Owen, the nineteenth-century social reformer and philanthropist, told the superintendents at his factories:

> *Many of you have long experiences in your manufacturing operations of the advantages of substantial, well-contrived and well-executed machinery. If, then, due care as to the state of the machinery can produce such beneficial results, what may not be expected if you devote equal attention to your animate machines, which are far more wonderfully constructed?*

In the twentieth century the preoccupation with mechanics has been replaced by one with organisations. Owen's plea remains appropriate even now.

The need to shift the emphasis away from the myopic view of managers as corporately driven pack animals is clear. All the research into how managers spend their time suggests that only a small percentage of their working day is actually spent on important tasks which achieve anything. It is estimated that conventional managers probably operate to just 40 per cent of their true ability. They spend 10 per cent of their time being really effective by doing what is important and 30 per cent gaining credibility in order to be really effective for that other 10 per cent. The rest of the time they spend doing things that are not important, or don't produce the outcome they want. Another study estimated that managers spend at least half of their time dealing with the consequences of bad decision-making.

Such estimates make salutory reading for managers who spend many hours every week at their desks – many more hours than they would actually need to spend if they were working to their full effectiveness.

THE RESEARCH

To learn more about the performance of individuals as managers, a number of senior managers were monitored over a prolonged period. They were not representative of any particular industry or managerial type. The monitoring did not concentrate on the minutia of their day but, instead, set out to track the development of their ideas, decisions, skills and performance – how strategy made the tortuous journey from an idea to reality. The work involved detailed discussion of how their ideas and policies developed, as well as their individual approaches to converting strategy into action. The resulting material included many hours of transcripted interviews which give an insight into the behaviour of individual managers in real situations.

The findings are striking and unique. Though involved in vastly different businesses and facing a wide variety of managerial challenges, there is a discernible link in the approach of the managers.

Central to their quest for high performance is what we have called the key simplicities. The key simplicities are intangible and unique to each individual manager – yet it appears that most managers make use of a number of them in their managerial style. The key simplicities are one of the means by which managers extract high performance from themselves, from their subordinates and from their organisations. There is no formula or catch-all phrase, such as empowerment, to describe the possibilities of the key simplicities. They are different techniques, some seemingly trivial, which allow managers to free themselves from the shackles of strategy and achieve high performance.

Key simplicities can involve an infinite variety of techniques and actions – using unusual but powerful images to communicate important strategic messages; insisting on one-page reports rather than lengthy theses; running meetings in a certain way. They involve intuition and commonsense, as well as a host of other aspects of personality.

There is no prescriptive route to success. 'There is no recipe for success, only failure,' says the guru of gurus, Peter Drucker. High performance is based on self-awareness and sensitivity to other people and the corporate environment, rather than the 'hard' and clearly defined skills normally ascribed to successful managers.

For managers who utilise the lessons from these high performers the benefits are potentially enormous. They can circumvent bureaucracy and exhaustively pointless policy making to concentrate on implementation and achievement.

High performers create situations, or allow themselves to be drawn into situations, where their strengths are needed. They are in the right place at the right time continually, able to escape from the mundanity of non-achievement. By recognising their own fundamental and individual strengths, they prove that there is a world of action and management beyond strategy.

Managers who recognise and use their skills to the full are rather like highly trained athletes. Hard work and practice has allowed them to master technique; apparently effortless, technique is invisible. The result is high performance.

Reference

1. D Quinn Mills, *Rebirth of the Corporation*, John Wiley, 1993.

1

HIGH PERFORMERS

The thoughts and actions of high performing managers were tracked over a number of months. In their own words, the managers explain how they convert ideas into action and action into achievement.

Putting vision to work
If vision is all important for corporate success how does the
visionary find a corporate role?

Making motivation happen
Managers motivate: QED. How one manager copes with the
fact that he could often do the job better than those he
delegates to.

Building on ambiguity
With certainty and security fast disappearing, a high
performer examines the new, ambiguous corporate order.

Strategy: from ideas to good habits
Overcoming habitual lethargy in a large company to translate
ideas into habitual high performance.

Networking to achieve change
The manager as the vital oil in the corporate engine of
change.

Gaining support in a multi-national
In a large organisation change is a slow process; the
ponderous movements of the luxury liner need now to be
replaced by the acceleration of the speedboat.

Working hard to inspire
Can the workaholic boss inspire others?

Thriving on complex projects
Faced with a huge international project, based in a jungle,
how can you make sense of it all?

Using uncertainty to build business
A manager explains how she copes with the uncertainty of
developing a new business through its fledgling days.

From public sector to public service
Transforming public sector management and organisation is
shaping to be one of the great managerial challenges of the
1990s. A manager at the sharp end of change looks at his role.

Our research started off with a lengthy interview with each manager. We talked about what he or she was currently doing. We then isolated several hazy ideas that had to be put into action. Together we then chose which one would be most appropriate to monitor. Ideas such as selecting a new divisional director or re-organising a department were rejected because they seemed too structured from the outset.

Instead we selected ideas which, at that time, were at little more than the conceptual stage. These included how to break down an organisation's existing regional identity and replace it with a sense of identity with newly formed territories; how to get staff to focus on relatively short-term financial issues without losing sight of longer-term aims and research opportunities; and how to bring people together in an inhospitable environment.

The managers were then monitored through regular and lengthy interviews over the following weeks and months. We wanted to avoid hearing them telling us history which, even in the most innocent of hands, has a habit of being embellished and re-written. Instead, we concentrated on the issues they faced at the time, those they anticipated and their plans to deal with them. The managers talked in-depth about how they approached problems and created strategies to bring long-term solutions.

Interestingly, all the high performers were successful in achieving their objectives, or were promoted or took on larger responsibilities, during or shortly after the tracking period.

What emerged was an insight into their approach to management and, more importantly, how they transformed strategy into action.

As many of the issues we talked of were sensitive and often personal, the names of the managers and their organisations have been disguised. What follows is – in their own words – their explanation of the way they worked. Each manager's comments are followed by analysis of the key points of their managerial technique.

PUTTING VISION TO WORK

The creative side of management has gained greater credence and acceptability over the last decade. Brainstorming is now an accepted activity; managerial visionaries increasingly find a place alongside managerial mechanics. Even so, there is still a suspicion that creativity rests uncomfortably with the practicalities of management and that vision is an indulgence.

In a crisis, it is argued, organisations do not require visions of the future but managers who are prepared to roll up their sleeves and get their hands dirty to extricate the company from the latest mire. Little thought is usually given to the fact that someone with new, perhaps unconventional, ideas might have averted the crisis in the first place or that inspiration is as valid a way forward as hard work.

Some managers make much of their creative input, building their careers around ideas as well as tangible achievements. One who has done this is John Charles, charged with retail development at a major UK building society. His job is to plan the strategy for the retail side of the business. Implementation occurs via a group of project managers who report directly to him. John regards himself as a person motivated and driven by his ability to come up with ideas. Ideas, creativity and vision are what makes management challenging for John.

I would love to be called a visionary. I get a real kick hearing about the visionary leaders in industry. Whatever industry they're in they can suddenly switch the battleground because they see things in a different light. They switch everything away from the opposition – so they don't even know it has happened and it might take them five years to work it out.

If I could have one of those sparks of genius in my life it would be enough for me.

I play chess and someone once said to me, you win at chess by not seeing the pieces as they are on the board. Everyone else looks at the board and says the knight can move from there to there, that will threaten this and that has an interaction with that. The way I look at it is, if that's a knight, what does the knight have, what are its unique characteristics, its unique strengths?

'I know its strengths intuitively – it can jump over other pieces. So where would I place it on the board? Where's the best strategic position to place it regardless of whether it can reach it now? Where feels good for a knight on the board?

'The chess board in my analogy represents the environment you find yourself in and the chess pieces are the characteristics, strengths, and skills you have to do certain things in certain situations. What I'm saying is: this is what I can do. I'm at this particular level in the organisation. I've got this amount of knowledge. I control this number of people. I've been on this business course, I've read this book and I've been exposed to these ideas or those ideas – they are all tangible things that have happened to me, that I've got now. How am I going to use them?

'My other way of thinking is to say: what are the natural strengths of that particular chess piece. What do I want to do with it? What would be the best position for me to be in? What's going to be the situation where I can really shine?

'That was a critical factor in how I got to where I am now in the organisation. There is a tacit agreement with my boss that I'll tell him any idea, no matter how stupid. Sometimes he'll tell me in no uncertain terms to go away. Three times out of ten, if I'm lucky, he'll say pursue it.

'I have, however, picked the ideas I've put to him very carefully. I've built a feeling of confidence because he's a very practical man and needs bottom-line benefits. In fact, a lot of the things I suggest don't have obvious bottom-line benefits, but are major problems for us.

'My strategy was gradually to grow my credibility, start with an issue that was fairly close to what he wanted. MIS was a good example. He wanted it so I gradually built a bigger and better MIS system. I would say why don't we measure how much business a supermarket down the road from one of our branches does? He would say, "Why the hell do I want to know that?" I would say because they are all customers, people walking up and down the High Street. I want him to ask me what he'd like to understand, what he would like to hear about.

'Six months ago if we had had conversations like that he would have kicked me out of the door. Now he's thinking about it seriously. That's the thing with all the areas I've moved into. I've used analogies and word pictures to take him on-board gradually.

'The mental image I have is of rolling countryside. The journey we've got to do is up and down those hills. But, if you go too far, you disappear out of sight in the next valley. And, if my boss can't see, he has no point of reference. So I can only take him a certain distance at each stage. I take him that distance then invite him to look back to where he's come from so he sees where his point of reference is. Then I say: "Now look forward. You see the hill up there, that's the next point we are going to get to." Then I take him on again. In between he's going to lose sight of me and what I am trying to achieve. But I've got to keep moving.

'When I have ideas it doesn't bother me if I can't pin them down. It doesn't concern me if I have no clear plan of action. I have a sort of inner reassurance that it will turn out fine. All this input goes in and there will be some sort of organic process in my head that filters it down and eventually reaches a stage where I understand and can act. I am intuitive and go with gut feeling. If something feels right I don't necessarily understand where it's taking me but it just feels right.

'A lot of people say that I go into things in too much depth, that I analyse and analyse to death. But I intuitively believe that you can go on and on peeling away the problems. It's like an onion, but you never reach the centre. When you peel away the last layer all you are left with is space. To get to the heart of the matter you've got to go on asking yourself questions and you've got to go on peeling. Now, the trouble is I don't usually have the time, forum or environment to do that.

'In chess there are two extreme schools of thought. The first says that it is a scientific game and, if you built a computer it would play chess better than any human. It would analyse all the positions and combinations. The second approach says that individuals don't analyse each line. It is not a game for computers. Sometimes we make sacrifices – we make a move because it looks and feels right. That's how people play – and that's how I manage. It is partly based on the experience of being in similar positions before. You remember what you did and if it worked. But it is also the fact that you can't analyse the situation completely. It feels right, you work down the path, you begin to see where it is leading and then you go there. That's the kind of thing I do when I'm trying to influence people. I try to think through what a course of action is going to be dealing with and then see how I can best use that. I cultivate the idea that I am a visionary so that people know I get some wacky ideas, but you have to be careful: some are real humdingers.'

Key points

The use of vision

John's sense of vision is something he has been aware of since leaving university. For him it is a way of life. There is always the suspicion that people full of ideas are not good at or interested in the implementation. John, however, is skilled at converting his vision into practical analogies and understands that his superiors and colleagues need to be taken along slowly.

Belief in self-knowledge

John has an in-built belief in his own ability to cut through thorny problems and emerge with an answer.

John's management style and the thinking which drives it are beyond imitation. Both are highly individual. What is striking is the depth of his awareness about how he operates. Despite time constraints, he seems to be able to find the space to think about what he wants to achieve at each stage (to this extent his approach is extremely logical).

Generating ideas

Constantly coming up with and seeking to implement new ideas is John's core philosophy. One of his key simplicities is his continual willingness to bring new ideas to old problems. He believes, passionately, in the power of ideas to bring about change.

Intuition

Married to all the other characteristics of John's management style is intuition. He trusts his own intuition and is prepared to step into the unknown if that is what it is telling him to do.

Managing the boss

Interestingly, his boss is viewed as a tool at John's disposal, someone to be guided along the route he has chosen rather than a creator of his own routes. John does not seek to disguise his ability to carry his boss along with him. Instead, he deliberately couches the idea in terms which he knows will appeal to his boss' preoccupation with bottom-line financial achievement. This could, perhaps, be seen as simple manipulation – even so, it is carefully thought out, a means of making sure John's ideas receive the most favourable hearing.

MAKING MOTIVATION HAPPEN

The ability of managers to motivate people is often assumed – like the ability of barristers to be good public speakers. The more senior you are in an organisation, the more people you have to motivate, yet as their careers progress managers receive little in the way of guidance or training. Given this, it is little wonder that so many of the big management ideas of the past have come to very little or nothing.

In a scathing attack on the fads of the 1980s, Quinn Mills says:

> *'Executives who talk of delegation, accountability, and risk-taking by subordinates generally know that they are not very successful at accomplishing these objectives. Much of what is proposed is not accomplished. Executives who say that the firm empowers workers and has transcended bureaucracy are merely dreaming.'*[1]

In reality, managers often struggle to pass on their enthusiasm for change or other ideas to their subordinates. Motives are one thing, motivation quite a different challenge.

Robert Dunn is marketing manager at an insurance company. His job involves working out a sales strategy and running a sales department of around thirty people. Central to his work and his success is his ability to motivate people to work to their full potential.

Candidly, he admits it isn't easy. After all, as a senior

manager you can do many of the jobs you delegate, often more effectively than the people who actually do them under your direction. It is a common problem. Patricia Scott, a director of taxation and treasury with Thorn EMI, says: 'If your boss doesn't see you doing things in the way he or she did them when they did your job, and they're not open-minded enough to concede that there are alternative methods, then you've got a problem.'[2]

So, how can you continue to motivate when, put simply, you could do a better job? Robert Dunn explains his approach.

'I think it's all about selecting the right tool for the right person according to the task you are asking them to do. I believe very much in letting them have ownership of the task. But, having said that, it depends on their relative experience. You either structure it for them or, if you think they have the experience and ability, you let them do it for themselves. If they do the latter you can coach them a little bit. Then, if they've got the ability to go further, you let them progress it and then finally, if you are very happy with them, let them delegate; you delegate it to them exclusively and just see what results come back.

'What hits you is that nobody does things the way you would have done. You always have a natural preference for the way you do it. Allowing people to do it their way, and accepting that the result isn't precisely what you would have done, is quite a test – particularly when you are developing new people in a new function. There's a temptation to want to do it yourself so you are always offering your organisation the very best standard. But that would be ridiculous because you'd never actually achieve anything.

'I can't remember who, but some philosopher said, "The best work is done by people if they think they've done it themselves." And while I can't quote the Chinese guy accurately, that sort of attitude has stuck with me. People feel a sense of achievement if they've done it. You may have guarded and guided them occasionally – whether you structured it at the beginning because you wanted them to see the way you felt it should go; just came in and coached them or tempered their frustration or lack of direction or whatever – but you have to say to them, "Yes, you are good enough. Do it your way."

'I suppose my unorthodox style is that people don't actually work for me. They work with me and I work with them. That's how I believe I can get the best performance out of individuals. I also give them collective direction so they can see how all the parts come together.

'More importantly I think you have to give people time. You won't find me rushing out of the door at five o'clock. If people want to talk to me we sit down and take whatever time is necessary. I think it's crucial and I think it's part of treating everyone on a level.

'I don't believe you get respect by demanding it. People will respect you if you are prepared to help when they need help, are prepared to give encouragement when appropriate and are prepared to give **constructive** criticism. That's something else that works, particularly when you are developing people. The way in which you give constructive criticism is important. People have to see the relevance of the things you want changed. You want them to feel that they are running the project but they have liaised and consulted with you.'

Key points

Situational leadership style

The emphasis Robert places on motivating others could be considered one of the key simplicities of his management style. It is regarded by him as the core of his job and one of his greatest attributes.

His approach is based on fundamental positive assumptions about the way people want to be led and managed.

Partnership

There is much talk of managers working in partnership with people. Robert is anxious that this is converted to action. In conversation, he used sporting analogies which stressed the importance of the combined team. Again, like motivation, partnership is something he has thought through and continually emphasises in practice.

BUILDING ON AMBIGUITY

'People want to be disciplined to feel part of a successful organisation. They need order. It is a virtuous circle,' WH Smith chairman, Sir Simon Hornby has observed.[3]

Traditionally, managers have set a great deal of store in this particular circle: security, discipline and clear authority succeeded and motivated simultaneously.

The circle – if it ever existed – is no more. The language of modern management is increasingly filled with the discomforting phraseology of our times. The old certainties have been replaced by insecurity about markets, the future of companies and the security of individuals.

On the macro scale, managers are confronted with paradigm shifts, discontinuity, and change in all its various manifestations. On a day-to-day personal front the phenomenon they continually face is ambiguity.

'The managerial process is messy. It is riddled with uncertainty and ambiguity. Managers cannot really predict the consequences of their actions, nor can their outcome be clearly identified,' says Jean-Louis Barsoux of Templeton College.[4]

Ambiguity is endemic and comes in many forms. Chiefly it can be found in uncertainty and confusion surrounding people's role in achieving change. The disappearance of hierarchies and, in particular, middle management has left managers in a strange situation. With fewer people surrounding and subordinate to them, managers are in something of an ambiguous vacuum. They must fill it or run the risk of being marginalised. The crucial question is how they view ambiguity and how they respond when they are confronted by it.

Mike Sutcliffe, a senior manager with a major bank, discussed how he utilises and makes the most of ambiguity. First, he considered how theory becomes practice in his organisation.

'I think what really matters in getting ideas into action is being very clear on what you really want. I don't think we're always very honest about saying, "I don't really know".

'Ideas become action because of commitment and energy. You pick people with a willingness to make things happen. You also need logic, internal coherence and consistency.

'Things get done because the obvious obstacles are dealt with. People don't agonise about it for too long. They're prepared to make decisions. And even if the decision takes them one step away from a solution, it's better to do that than sit around and worry about it.

'People need to have a positive "We can do it" kind of approach. They can't be afraid. They should actively want to do something, because they experience a sense of fun and achievement. When I look at why things don't get done, it's because people without much direction are looking after them, because senior people take their eyes off the ball, because there's no fun, joy or sense of kudos attached to the work.

'Often it comes down to the question of whether these managers are people who can actually change things. If, as a manager, you can't bring about change then you are unlikely to achieve a great deal. Some managers do things that really suit them and not much else. And then there are those who are prepared to do something new, something different, something interesting. They are most likely to respond to challenges.

'People are often rather confused and don't really know what's going on or what is important. We are trying to bridge the gap between the executives and the managers; the ideas and the practice. We're actually trying to get people to enter that void. Rather than managers going back, which is always a danger, and start spelling it out, we're trying to get more people to fill that gap, accept responsibility, and for us to sort out the ragged edges.

'The situation is filled with ambiguous grey areas. A lot of people learn to control their reactions to ambiguity and appear to be tolerant because they manage to keep the stress it induces under control. They'd sooner not have it, but can cope with it. And then there are a number of people who quite clearly fall apart at the big open space created by ambiguity. They feel it is personally threatening. A lot of people define themselves by what they do. If that isn't very clear, then they feel very unclear about themselves.

'You can also have complete ambiguity of role. I think you can get to the point where it is unclear what you are meant to be actually creating. The human resource textbooks tell you to spend a lot of time getting role clarity, but sometimes role ambiguity can be quite useful. The highest level of role ambiguity I ever came across was consulting. Are you a parent, teacher, mentor or guide?

'When a person's individual role is very ambiguous, they sometimes become very insecure and upset, especially if the normal channels of power and position are being taken away from them and certain relationships are changing. That can be very threatening. They can be terribly assertive, abrasive and directive, struggling for certainty.

'Obviously, living with, tolerating and thriving on ambiguity is not common. People carry on with the belief that there is a right answer. The trouble is I don't think you can measure progress when you are dealing with ambiguity. I think you just have to say, "I've got this problem. I'll think about it, I'll do that and I'll go and talk to him about it." I think you have to throw ideas at the problem. I sit down with a piece of paper and work out all the things I need to do and what I have done so far. As I do it, I can feel it getting easier.

'You need to clarify what you actually understand, what you're trying to find out and then clarify the resources to be used to solve things. I think you can do that with a fairly high level of staff and with a fairly high level of problem.

'You say to yourself, "I know there's hardly anything that can tell me whether I'm right or wrong." You can try logic, but often it doesn't work. There's nothing going to tell you whether your hunch will succeed. So you might as well get on with it and follow your hunch and see what happens. The first thing is to have the courage to actually sit down and say, "Let's experiment a bit and see what happens."

'The second thing is to be good at experimental design. You can't say, "I just can't do it," and hope everything will be fine. You end up creating the same mess again. You've got to say, "I believe this is right. Now I've got to find out what actually matters within the solution." You go from a very wide focus to a very tight focus.

'You also find ambiguity in terms of personal position, which I find hardest to cope with. You find yourself saying, "How do I stand in relation to what's happening there or in relation to that person?" And, of course, for the board of directors, that is about personal power and personal position. I think if you create too much personal ambiguity about issues like that, you can create a lot of problems.

'There is also intellectual ambiguity – three or four different people telling you the same thing. You're not sure if you've got very good data. Then you have to decide if all the data is really saying the same thing, or whether you should search for more data.

'You often see people trying to impose order on a situation where it's just not possible. Typically, as soon as you start to lose control of a situation, certain kinds of people will try to reinforce the existing order and will become more and more draconian as they try to regain the control they once had. They lack the flexibility to say, "Hold on, things have changed completely." So they go off into their totalitarian response which just worsens things. People who can deal with ambiguity say, "Well the normal ways of dealing with this have disappeared. I can't rely on what's gone on in the past, those sort of responses aren't working. What can we do and what do we know, however imperfectly, about the new situation? How can we try to mould it towards where we want to get to?"

'Also, I think some people deliberately seek out ambiguity or create ambiguity because they find it personally stimulating and are very creative in these situations. Or perhaps it gives them some political or power advantage. Those are the people who tend to abuse information.'

Key points

Clarity and honesty

Mike's management style is continually to seek out clarity – of purpose and action. Only with such clarity does he believe change can be brought about. Central to this is honesty. He wants managers to be honest enough with themselves and their colleagues to admit to ambiguity, vagueness and weakness. Only then can people move on to learn from what they do, rather than repeating the same mistakes again and again.

Thriving on uncertainty

Admitting that there is a problem is often half the battle in achieving a cure. Mike acknowledges that status, position and situation are now unlikely to be as clearcut as they once were. While striving for clarity, he is prepared to accept that it cannot always be achieved. He is brutally realistic, but still retains his optimism about management's ability to achieve change.

Confidence in judgement

As with other high performers, Mike is sure of his judgement and reading of situations. This confidence is, however, hard earned. He is constantly prepared to ask questions, to challenge assumptions, in order to ensure that his judgement is backed up. This approach does not make management any easier – opinions inevitably vary.

STRATEGY: FROM IDEAS TO GOOD HABITS

When starting a new job managers are often full of optimism. They believe that they have identified areas where improvements could be made and are anxious – often overly anxious – to bring about change. In most cases their initial enthusiasm is soon dissipated as they face entrenched interests and habits; colleagues and subordinates uninterested in doing things differently.

Some managers, through a combination of undying optimism, pig-headedness, arrogance and commitment, succeed in shaking the corporate tree and are able to turn their ideas into reality. Along the way their idealism inevitably becomes tempered, but new ideas can be converted into habitual behaviour.

David Andrews is an economics and planning manager with a multinational corporation. Beginning a new job, he set out to change the way things were done.

'I've got a lot of enjoyment and quite a kick out of trying to re-focus our objectives. It's not that we didn't have strategies before, but I wanted to look at them again and bring them up to date. I wanted to convert our strategies into a process in which our operating companies in the four corners of the Earth could play a part. I argued that it is no good doing an exercise like this – where you update your objectives, strategies and discuss what the issues are and get all this stuff sorted out – and then all you do is publish a beautiful report. To me it would be completely futile if you don't get out there and talk to the people who are actually running the business. After all, they are the people who have their hands on the levers. In practice, we don't run anything. They are taking the decisions that are supposed to be implementing these strategies.

'A basic tenet of faith in this company was that the operating companies were key and that the chief executive of each carried the responsibility. He didn't report to the central head office but to his regional manager. The central head office had no direct authority apart from deciding on the next jobs people took.

'We examined the plans of the operating companies and decided whether they were technically sound or not. Basically, we added up a list of apparently reasonable things and checked that the sum total wasn't unrealistic.

'The process had being going on from time immemorial to everyone's satisfaction. But, when I took my job I said I wasn't prepared to be a corporate bean counter. I wanted to go through the process in much more depth.

'My boss agreed. I think he knew what was coming, but he didn't let on and I guess that was his way of protecting himself. I decided we would review our business worldwide in real depth. We would use the process of making the review and presenting it to top management and then taking it to the operating companies to change the frame of reference for the people out there running the business.

'First I needed to sort out in my own mind what I thought our objectives and broad strategies were. Then I planned to go to the chief executives and put the story across to them and their management team. What I was saying was here's a view of what the issues are, our worldwide and group objectives, and some ways of thinking about our business.

'I was aware of a number of areas where we should have been doing things that we weren't. But largely I didn't know how the strategy would emerge. Some things were not well expressed in the organisation, we did not have a language for them but, as we went through the review, I learned a tremendous amount.

'Some would say this was all a waste of time. But, I believe it actually makes a difference. You would never be able to measure it apart from hints that people are doing things a little differently – the way they start to express their programmes, the way they talk about the profitability of their companies. The great thing about talking to people who are actually running businesses is that if they hear a good idea they snatch it and tell their people they've invented it.

'I persuaded my boss to back the review and I announced it to the group of managing directors. This was crucial. Once you've committed yourself you have to go ahead and, much more important, my boss was committed. It was agreed that I wouldn't just sit there and invent what we were going to do. Instead I met with a selection of managers to brainstorm what should be in the report.

'We identified a focal person in each section who would be responsible for collecting all the data. We had a kind of underground network of people further down the organisation. We then presented it to the top managers. It was interesting because I think if we hadn't had the commitment created by going public, the review would have stopped at that meeting. We were proposing to provide good data on every major parameter for each of the businesses. My idea was that if you could provide it in a way that was completely transparent, the necessary actions would scream out from the data. If you've got a book of analysis that shows that a business is bottom of the league tables in everything, there's nowhere for anyone to hide.

'The two most senior managers, who could see what was coming, tried their best to kill it off. There was a rear guard action, but my boss supported me and we moved on.

'The challenge of the first four months was to get agreement that we would actually do this exercise. Then it was difficult to get good data from each of the operating units. My technique was to use people whom I knew were owed some favours by many of the units and get them to call some of those favours in. I was also helped because there are many engineers and scientists in our organisation and, whatever the politics, scientists always prefer good clean data. This worked to my advantage. We decided to capture in a single report a review of all of our country operations. It was the first time that this had been done though it turned out my boss had been trying to do it for years.

'I view our business as a jewel, a diamond. We were going to look at the diamond from every possible direction and in every direction another picture would emerge. We looked at the business against just about every variable that we could think of. It was a hell of an effort. But we were forcing people to look at the world, our place in it, the competition and our position relative to them.

'Having looked at our total business we then said let's write down what we think our total strategies are. I wrote exactly what I believe – our strategies are judged by what we actually do, not what we say we do. We inspected our strategies and identified the things we were doing to our satisfaction and those we were not.

'What emerged was that with the strategies that had been in place a long time, we were doing well. They were part of our normal way of doing business. But the relatively new strategies, those that had come up in the last year or two, often had no true commitment. The strategy was not being fulfilled. There were clear gaps.

'It may be difficult to get large organisations to do things – in the same way it is difficult to get a decent tune on a large church organ – but the thing about big organisations, and especially our sector, is that it is entirely predictable. Once you have established a way of doing things then the system is predictable. If it's not kept up to standard it will tend to rot but, once taught, it will replicate easily.

'By the time the report was circulated, we had achieved a collective commitment from all the top managers to our aims and strategies. This of course was immensely important in an organisation of our size.

'I then arranged to visit every operating business around the world with a one-day seminar. Everyone enjoyed the opportunity to give feedback. This sort of process was a first. And everyone liked to be told there was a grand plan – they'd never seen any direct evidence of it before! We said, "We are here to show you the framework of our thinking and not to tell you what to do." Some were disappointed that the plan seemed very loose.

'If you take all the top managers in our group (about 45 people) I'm sure you will find there are a few who are dyed in the wool. For them this whole process has had little effect. But if you take some of the younger people who are just coming into these top jobs, they are powerfully energised by the whole exercise.

'The process has merely amplified the feedback mechanisms that already existed. People always used to 'phone each other and exchange ideas. We collected all these messages to ensure that everyone received the same high quality data.'

Key points

Building good habits

Summing up his technique, the snooker player Steve Davis explained: 'Perfect cueing, up and down like a piston, always straight, always the same. The balls are irrelevant. They're just confirmation that what I'm doing is right.' David's approach is somewhat similar.

His aim is to develop habits throughout the organisation which are unaffected by local or corporate pressure – standard ways and means of looking at strategic issues. Once the habits are in place, David believes that the right results will occur naturally every time.

Playing to strengths

David creates situations or allows himself to be pulled into situations where his strengths are needed. He is acutely aware of his weaknesses and avoids situations where that lack of skill would let him down.

Knowing the organisation

It seems an obvious point, but David is unusually aware of the nature of the organisation he works for. He has an acute sense of the organisation's size and ponderous character. Rather than becoming exasperated at this, he recognises the timescales involved in achieving change and alters his objectives and schedule accordingly.

Using the organisation

David is a natural rebel. When consultants were supposed to be allowed into his meetings he threw them out, despite being relatively junior. He delights in telling how he told off his boss for wanting some data earlier than the promised delivery date. Yet, he obviously has an ability to convince his managers that they should tolerate this rebelliousness. Somehow he doesn't frighten them. Other managers who acted in the same way would undoubtedly make the board feel uncomfortable; David carries on.

What David does, in effect, is to control and develop people's expectations of him, the organisation and, ultimately, themselves.

'Ultimately there is no agreed version of effectiveness,' says Jean-Louis Barsoux of Templeton College. 'It is driven, not by the logic of the job, but by the expectations. Effectiveness is about identifying the people that matter, establishing a restricted number of high expectations and being seen to fulfil those expectations.'[5] This is an apt summary of how David Andrews converts strategy into practice.

NETWORKING TO ACHIEVE CHANGE

For the manager in the 1990s, managing change is a fundamental skill. While most managers would accept the necessity for change, many find it difficult to establish their own role in the process.

It is all too easy for senior managers to become distanced from the real implications of changes in outlook, strategy and practice. Rather than becoming participants they can become benign commentators, ever ready with the sound bite but lacking in corporate bite.

Don Lord is editorial director of a group of local news-papers. Like many other companies in the media industry, his organisation has been going through a process of rapid change. Don describes how he tries to fulfil his role in the change process.

'Though we have changed the organisation greatly, many of the journalists haven't moved very much at all. A lot of them joined the company and have stayed throughout their careers. We have to sell them the need to change so they realise that the company's culture also has to change. The thing is you don't make just a single change and that's it, the paper's alright now. It's never right. It's a living organism, just like anything else. It's part of society and, as society changes, it has to reflect those changes all of the time.

'One thing I do, perhaps once a month or so, is deal with the 20 or 30 letters I've received complaining about the quality of the paper, mistakes, bad printing, or torn papers. These come from a whole range of customers, so I ring them up and talk to them about their complaint. It has a wonderful effect. They think it's tremendous that I've taken the trouble to talk to them. I can't do it every day because I don't have the time but it has a lot of value in terms of personal contact and word gets around on the grapevine.

'I respond similarly if one of my staff says, "I was talking to someone and they're complaining about such and such and are going to cancel the newspaper." I get their 'phone number, call them and find out the problem and how I can help. I do this because if I'm out of touch with why customers are discontented, I am unable to make changes which will keep them as customers. I've got to be involved and it's quite fun as well.

'Looking back over the last five years in particular, when much has changed, the words which come to mind are oil and lubricant, the things that make everything happen. I suppose that's one of the reasons why I've been able to implement a lot of changes. We've redesigned both our papers and all our weekly titles, we've looked at the costings of our weekly titles, different sorts of changes, in fact, the whole bag of tricks. The changes have been warmly accepted by both readers and advertisers which is great. I think the way I have been able to bring about change – or introduce change enthusiastically – is by getting people on my side.

'I see my role as lubricating the wheels of the business. Change focuses on people. If they can see the good sense in what you're doing they support it. It's not a matter of looking at the hierarchy and then selecting them. It's a question of picking out the opinion formers from among the teams and helping them to understand the value of what you're doing. They can then sell it to everyone else. You don't just do that with your own department, you do it to other departments as well. It is a very good investment of time. It is what is fashionably called networking. I didn't realise I did a certain amount of networking – but I realise now, it is the way to get things through.'

Key points

Change

It is one thing accepting the need for change, quite another to be able to look at it objectively and continually as an on-going process. Don is highly involved in the change programme, but remains objective.

Customer service

Ringing customers is an old trick. But, how many senior managers actually do it? Not many have the commitment – or perhaps the courage – to go directly to the people who matter. Don regards it as a simple means of keeping in touch with the concerns of customers and of demonstrating his fundamental commitment to achieving, rather than simply talking about, genuine change.

Networking

Don's objectivity allows him to identify likely barriers to change and to identify the key opinion formers. His rejection of hierarchy as the best means of determining someone's influence is interesting – he, after all, works with and probably chose many of the people he circumvents. This is a risky strategy, unless you are very sure of your judgement. It could be seen as undermining the position of some managers. It does, however, work for him.

GAINING SUPPORT IN A MULTI-NATIONAL

Achieving change in a large and complex organisation is a slow process, but one that needs to be speeded up if the organisation is to remain competitive.

Ken Lawrie heads a division within a multinational chemical company. Intent on achieving change, he has adopted a highly personal approach. In the age of empowerment and partnership, he aims to get people on his side by involving them directly in the process of strategy formulation. Talking to us, he mapped out his aims and his methods.

'The business was not focused narrowly enough. We needed to re-focus our people so that staff around the world bought into the idea of a new strategy. It was a hard message to sell – we have to deliver today as well as promising jam for tomorrow – and I had to confront some of the sacred cows of the business. I had to convince people that not all parts of the business are strategically equal while still showing commitment to growing the business. I needed my ideas to be owned by people without having vast numbers of managers flying around the world to convince them.

'Running big successful organisations is a hard slog. They don't become that way overnight. It involves gaining credibility and commitment. I knew where I wanted the business to go and the resources we needed, but I was not sure that the main board would give me a favourable hearing. To make it happen, I planned a series of group meetings and I spent time talking to everyone about the implications of the strategy. I didn't want it to be an enormous shock to them, but for them to feel part of the process. Once a week, I talked to most of the people who run the company, using the 'phone a lot, circulating documents about the strategy before the final draft and travelling a great deal to maintain more informal conversations. I find it useful to travel with people so they have the opportunity to talk. I also get my secretary to button-hole key people. This is a crucial part of gaining ownership and influence.

'You can tell if people have belief in the strategy if they are prepared to discuss it. They want to understand, have an input and see it as a logical step forward. Also, people are prepared to put their concerns on the table. Good decisions are pretty self-evident with obvious logical components. Other decisions are only good if they have the will of the people and commitment.

'As part of the process, I think about things that have gone badly. I think about why they have gone wrong. I talk to people I trust about these things so I have a fairly meticulous plan with things mapped out. It may sound vague but, for me, it is meticulous. You've got to spend time with enthusiastic, committed people, explaining why some ideas are carried through and what they should be thinking. It's like coaching.

'No single person coaches me, but in reality everyone does. My managers criticise presentations and help me to get it right.

'In the end, the strategy book we worked on involved everyone's thinking. One of the managers in Australia was sent every paper for his comments – this got him totally involved so he understood the international nature of the proposals and was able to contribute. By and large I influenced the thinking and synthesised it, getting to a position where people own it and accept the obligations of the strategy.

'The information in the book should drive us. Once you've got all the information together, you are pushed to some obvious conclusions about where you stand in the business and what needs to be done to be successful. And out of these details falls the content of the strategy.

'In a large corporation, you don't actually make a dramatic change in strategy. It's like the Queen Mary turning – you do it very slowly. And, if you describe it, it sounds like a jumble. If someone asked me if I had systematically planned all that had happened the answer is, no I didn't. There are a lot of separate strands which naturally come together as well as bits of work started at different times.

'It's really just a matter of presenting a very complex issue as simply as possible and then discovering when you present it simply that you don't like the answer yourself!

'You end up with a nicely prepared document which is strategy, which is out of date from the day it was written, because it's about uncertainty and being able to cope with uncertainty. The process of getting to that document, particularly with a very decentralised organisation without a big central staff, is much more about talking to people and getting them committed to the broad direction of the business and the broad issues of research allocation, rather than getting commitment to forecasts to the nearest penny. It is necessarily a disorganised process.

'One of our companies has a central team that puts together a strategic model. They try out the strategic model on people in the field. But the last one was not owned by anyone. People started out by saying we can't achieve that, you've imposed it on us, we don't want it.

'What I try to do is produce something people feel comfortable with and feel they want a role in. It might not deliver exactly what they want but they believe it's achievable, sensible, and well thought through and communicated. The trouble is the process of communication is often untidy.'

Key points

Making it simple

Ken has an automatic desire to express things simply and to reduce grand strategic plans to simple ideas which can be easily communicated. In fact, he regards distilling down complexity as a critical part of his job. He is the synthesiser of other people's data, information and opinions.

Getting close to people

As well as taking prime responsibility for effective communication, Ken invests substantial amounts of time in one-to-one contact with his colleagues and subordinates. Air travel is regarded by him as a key opportunity to talk freely (this point was also made by the other managers). He allocates generous amounts of time to getting to know new managers: he is not being sociable; he wants them to participate and share knowledge and insight.

Becoming a contributor

At a meeting Ken was quite happy not to be in the chair. Instead, he listened and contributed frequently without attempting to dominate. In fact, he appears more comfortable in this role – one of a team rather than as an isolated figurehead.

Seeking ownership

The word ownership was key to Ken's entire outlook. He wanted strategy to be understood, supported by and involving everyone. On a research project he insisted that people from a number of units were involved. It wasn't strictly necessary and annoyed the head of research, but Ken was adamant that people needed to be involved directly if their colleagues were to support the project. At every stage, he tried to keep people involved – the Australian manager, for example, was kept meticulously up to date with the latest progress on the strategic plan because he had something to contribute and would be instrumental in making it work.

Accepting the muddle

The complexity of strategy-making and making things happen in a large organisation does not deter Ken. He accepts that there are blind alleys and that the end result is often not as clinical as you imagined. He is a pragmatist, willing to accept a small advance or even a setback if it brings him closer to his goal.

Reviewing mistakes

In a very political company, Ken seeks out people he trusts so that he can learn from his mistakes. Despite being a very forceful character he is constantly willing to learn. His entire management technique is built around being open – if he is honest with himself and his colleagues, he believes they will recriprocate.

WORKING HARD TO INSPIRE

We have all met workaholics who seem to spend every hour of every day working. Richard Webster, chairman of a large engineering company, is one of them. He believes his example and enthusiasm are key motivating factors in his business.

'I am a person who exudes enthusiasm, so one problem I've never had is motivating people. I've always worked very long days, worked hard and effectively, and I've always, always been very proud of everybody in the team who've done exactly the same – giving their all. Automatically they do everything that is asked of them – they've worked any amount of hours, weekends, nights, any time. I think it's because, although I wasn't always conscious of it, but have been for the last few years, I'm an enthusiastic sort of person and enthusiasm is very contagious. It's a great asset that I've only recently realised I've got. With enthusiasm, people sort of get on board and, I think, that's really quite powerful.

Working with people is the most important thing I do.

'I believe if someone comes to work for me I pay them well and expect them to give me their absolute. I don't believe you should tell people to do things. You should ask them and they should expect to come in early every morning and go home late at night and just work and work because they enjoy doing it.

'If I 'phone someone tonight and say I want to meet them somewhere tomorrow morning and then we're going to work until seven at night I expect them to do it. And they all do, without hesitation.

'The people who don't fit in with the team and cause problems tend to be the type who write letters. I mean if my directors write to each other they get in trouble because why should you ever want to write to someone in the same building as you? What you do is walk into their office and say, "What the hell are you doing? Explain it to me." You don't write something sarcastic. The people who do are normally quite weak. I want them to go in and say, "Look we've got a problem, what the hell are you doing that for?" In this industry you do what you think is right – and then you discuss it.'

Key points

Commitment

Richard invests a daunting amount of energy into his work and expects the same of others.

Communication

Richard communicates in a direct way with no ceremony or pretence. He takes the risk of hurting others – and perhaps himself – to make sure his message is consistent.

Personnel selection

Richard chooses people who can cope with this very demanding way of working. Perhaps he is able to do so because he clearly describes how he works and is consistent and honest in his approach.

THRIVING ON COMPLEX PROJECTS

Few, if any, managers would deny that their jobs and the environments in which they operate have, over the last few years, become ever more complex. They find themselves having to cope with more international problems than ever before; established industries are in a state of turmoil, as are many organisations; and they have continually to keep up to date with new technology.

Dealing with complexity has become an integral part of managerial work. Previously projects offered a simplifying way through such complexity. They were clear cut and tightly defined – building a bridge was a project. Today, projects are also afflicted by increased complexity. They are bigger than ever before, last longer, involve more people and, more often than not, have an international component.

Karl-Heinz Muller is a project manager in a major

European engineering company. The project he was managing when we spoke, was one of huge complexity. Senior manager with a consortium of four organisations working on a South American chemical plant, he was dealing with the various needs of the consortium members and the changing demands of the client. He was also handling the day-to-day tribulations of creating a turnkey chemical plant within two years, in a hostile climate with nearly 100 per cent humidity and harsh working conditions.

'My *raison d'être* is to look at the time, money and technology in the project.

'You start with an ideal of how the project is to be executed. Though, in our terms this is not a very big project, the pressure to meet deadlines is immense and there are penalties if we are late which would wipe out any profits. Month to month, we are paid on our progress – physical progress is financial progress. I have to predict and prove what we've done every month.

'To give you an idea – there are 2,000 technical drawings for the plant and it generates 400,000 statistics every month. I can only spend money if I can prove a particular approach doesn't work. Each single item we buy is broken down into six stages which the client then examines and approves. Out of this I have to produce a manageable system.

'It is hard. I am working a 16-hour day, moving between South America and Germany. I haven't even had time to learn Spanish and there is certainly no time for friendship in this business. During the execution of the project there is zero satisfaction. The client started off continually saying we could do better. Sometimes they were writing a letter a day with a complaint or question.

'In this project I am an ambassador, but engineers are not diplomats, they concentrate on technique and money. I am used to jobs where you have to keep different people satisfied and with this project I know that if I reach a point where our client says "no", they mean it. I have to find another solution. I have to be a diplomatic engineer.

'We are dealing with different cultures – of working and living. We have to sell our approach to the client. As things have progressed, the client has become a lot easier and is now willing to learn and realises that we, as Europeans, are prepared to compromise. They know they are not getting a cheap plant. We are trying to build a plant which is state of the art.

'Our client is used to dealing with American companies which have a completely different approach to managing such projects. The American way of doing things is hiring people for the job and then firing them. There is no transfer of experience and knowledge. This means we have had to do a lot more training than planned. American process control is also very detailed, but this is not the German approach. I have a rough idea of where we stand day by day – an American would know exactly.

'In a consortium you also have the problem of diluted responsibility. It is difficult to deal with some of the other partners. They are looking after their own ends all the time. One of them knows nothing about building a chemical plant. Partners often don't actually work as partners, but as sub-contractors. Even so, I have to be available to our consortium partners. They are forbidden to talk to the client. I am their mouthpiece. And, as the major partner, I also have to defend our company's interests. But our partners aren't interested in support. They are looking for a fall back so they can say "we told you so".

'Sometimes, dealing with our partners takes up half of my time but, usually, I work for one week a month on my report on progress; one week dealing with our partners and only two weeks working on the project. I meet with the management team every week, but spend a lot of time looking at what has been done rather than what needs to be done.

'Dealing with the clients and partners means that I spend a lot of time writing. The procurement people write two letters a day to me. Getting all the paper together for the client is a big problem. If the client has a question I have to find an answer agreed by all the partners. The spoken word doesn't count. It has to be written so everyone can refer to it.

'This means there is no time available for me to give support and help on the engineering side though I still have to define problem areas, suggest corrective actions and push them through.

'There are many other aspects of this project. The legal and bureaucratic system here is very flexible so you have to know how to use it. A hurricane hit one of our supply vessels so that caused more problems. Then there are the working conditions. Morale goes up and down from day to day. There have been strikes. The German workers stayed in their hotel when the air conditioning on the site stopped working – it was soon fixed.

'To keep these sort of problems to a minimum, I spend a lot of time trying to find the right people. I ask people if they've worked with them before and ask on site if they will work with the new recruit.

'The people are not always easy to work with. We have

instrumentation engineers who are very specialised. They are
very arrogant and difficult to monitor. Others who are
working on site are used to having very tight controls. They
are too automated in their approach.

'On top of this I have also been training my successor which
eats into my time and makes jobs last a little longer than they
should.

'Every month there is another problem which you didn't
know would emerge. No one had checked the fire-fighting
plans for the plant. They turned out to be poor quality.
Sometimes it is the client who has people supervising our
work, who spots a potential problem. I also have co-
ordinators for engineering, construction and procurement.

'If I think something is not quite right I ask for a small
report on that specific area. The trouble is that I might be in
Germany rather than on site when I see something in our
monthly report which concerns me – we have four offices
dealing with this project.

'Often you can't be face-to-face with the people on site.
Talking by telephone is complicated by the South American
phone system and the time difference. What we do is send
short faxes. If I write down a problem it becomes clearer. The
same applies to my people – if they have a problem they write
it down and send it to me. The engineers are usually working
on other projects so they don't have much time. The faxes are
handwritten, they can be done quickly, and people can write
in German rather than English which is their second
language. If you ask the right questions at the right time and
in the right way you usually get the problem solved. We also
have a meeting every couple of weeks at which anyone can
bring up a problem they've come across or see arising as we
progress. There is no come back so people have a chance to

get problems out in the open.

'I was never a very patient person and sometimes on this project I have exploded. I need a day off every week so I make sure I take it easy on Sunday. I have to do something different.'

Key points

Communications

With four offices in Germany and South America the logistics of communicating on this project were daunting. Karl-Heinz is, however, unperturbed by the fact that serious problems could arrive when he is thousands of miles away.

He recognises official communication as a necessary evil, a means of keeping the client fully informed on every detail and keeping his partners content. Karl-Heinz sees this as a diplomatic activity – the filling of filing cabinets rather than something of assistance to the project. Nevertheless, he made sure this formal communication was kept up.

His method of communication with colleagues short-circuited cumbersome reports and political machinations. If he is concerned he asks for a 'small report'. Managers on site then produce concise, hand-written résumés of the situation in German. Their thoughts are clarified and Karl-Heinz can either take it further or forget his concerns. This technique simplifies complex processes and problems and, more importantly, solves them.

Clear idea of his role

Karl-Heinz has an exceptionally clear vision of what he is capable of doing and what he needs to do in any particular situation. He recognises the politics played by his partners and client, but seeks to play no part in them.

In general terms he knows the project would not necessarily fall to pieces without him and sees his role as intervening to solve problems, smooth over difficulties and prevent problems happening in the first place.

Using the organisation

Geographically isolated, Karl-Heinz makes full use of his own organisation. If there is a problem which he knows his superior would be able to help him with he asks for assistance and support immediately – it is always forthcoming.

Finding the right people

With skills shortages and highly complex projects, recruitment is growing in importance – not least because the cost of selecting the wrong person is now extremely high. 'We look at recruiting with the same kind of intensity as we do discovering new molecules in the lab,' says the head of worldwide marketing at a major drugs company.

Karl-Heinz is similarly preoccupied and precise as to the people he needs. They are not always available and part of the challenge for Karl-Heinz is to free colleagues from other assignments to work with him. He invests a great deal of time and effort – not to mention air miles – attempting to find the right people. He uses his knowledge of his own organisation to free the people, and also smooths the way by checking their record and temperament with others on site and in Germany.

USING UNCERTAINTY TO BUILD BUSINESS

The fledgling days of a new organisation are often wracked with unforeseen difficulties. Uncertainty abounds. Catrina Carlberg is managing director of a new off-shoot from a major telecommunications company. When we talked, she was seeking partners for the year-old company and was on the verge of an agreement with a Dutch organisation. She was dividing her time between Stockholm and Amsterdam, planning the company's worldwide launch and establishing a Dutch base.

'Ours is a new business so the future is still uncertain. I like the uncertainty of our business. Not every single person who works for me shares this view, but the majority do. Perhaps when the business grows it will be different.

'I talk to people a lot about what they want to do and achieve. I try to travel with people because then you talk all the time. It's the best way of understanding them. They are not afraid to talk about things they wouldn't normally talk about.

'The challenge of running a small company like this is that, as a knowledge-based organisation, we need to be informal and work as a team even though we now have more than one location. We are too small to be two companies so people must feel they belong and can contribute.

'Over the last year I've spent about 20 per cent of my time maintaining the business and the remainder developing it for the future – hiring new staff, talking to prospective partners. Creating something is exciting – in my last job I spent most of my time maintaining the business.

'Working for a big company, my diary was booked three to four months ahead. Meetings were planned for me by others, imposed on me. Now, my diary is blank. With a small company – we now have ten people – you need just one meeting a week and that's enough. We also have one planning day a month, checking prospects and our priorities. I admit, I am a very bad administrator, and perhaps I should plan a little bit better. It is a reaction against having your future mapped out so strictly.

'I remember that I was impressed when I spoke to companies like IBM where people always had the time to meet me. I try to do that. If a client wants to see me I need to be there – if it is Washington or anywhere. Some people become irritated if they find I am in Amsterdam – I don't even know myself if I will be in Amsterdam tomorrow – but you need to develop relationships with customers.

'I need to think every morning what is the important thing to do. Other things happen so I keep the crucial things down to two hours.

'If I am faced with a decision and have no information I do nothing. I wait. I can't force myself to take a decision. It is a question of opening your mind to impressions. If I get into a problem I often remember a similar situation in the past and think how I or someone came up with a solution. How you get it I don't know. The past is your database, like a picture book. You match the patterns you see before you to your mental picture book. You may not have thought about something before, but somehow you find that you know it already.

'Often if something is important, you know exactly what you need to do. If I am looking for a solution, I talk to people whom I think might be able to help. It's not formal – I don't go to a boss. Often I talk to people who have nothing to do with the business, people I trust. Eventually, I say, yes I have come to a decision.

'When I feel something is going well I then deal with something which isn't running smoothly. With children you leave them alone if they are playing happily. It is the same with a company. Being able to leave things alone is important.

'Sometimes you think you don't want to think about the job for another second – then the 'phone rings. But, I tell myself when I've had enough. I can sit down and cut myself off.

'The reward for all this is getting things to work, making them happen. It is important to decide how you reward yourself. I think, now, I enjoy myself 80 per cent of time against 50 per cent in my previous job. It's not a question of money. I want to be able to have an impact on things. I don't want to be an important person myself – if I did, I would have stayed with a big company where there's more status.

'At the moment we are building our credibility. I know what I want to do with the company, the overall direction, but things change. The opening up of Eastern Europe altered our short-term objectives. It became an opportunity. That was not part of our strategy. But, you have to accept it when these things come about.

'I think if you believe in an idea you have to carry on and

never take no for an answer. After all, it is always easy for people to say no. You have to be true to yourself – don't pretend to be something you are not.'

Key points

Trusting judgement

Catrina has a great deal of quiet, unspoken confidence in her judgement. For a major launch at an international conference she left the arrangements to a young manager she had little knowledge of. Despite the launch's huge importance, Catrina only attended four meetings, such was her certainty about her own judgement.

Confidence without data

During the time we talked to Catrina she made little mention of having a boss. There was never an impression that there was a superior whom she had to keep happy or whose expectations she had to meet. Indeed, it was only after persistent questioning she admitted to having people she reported to. The details of reporting arrangements remained vague. Yes, she saw the overall chairman every few months but, as the launch approached and plans became finalised she only met her boss on one occasion. It appeared she had the confidence to continue to do what she thought was right. There was no need in her mind to seek confirmation or to clarify roles in the new organisation.

FROM PUBLIC SECTOR TO PUBLIC SERVICE

For managers in the public sector, the 1990s pose huge managerial challenges. Central to the process of change is the transformation of many government bodies from monopolistic and bureaucratic monoliths into market-driven service organisations.

The scale of the changes are unprecedented. Tentatively and controversially, an entirely new culture is being developed in enormous organisations. One of the managers making it happen is John Michaels, head of a territory in a large government department with 75,000 staff as well as 2,000 centrally based policy-makers. His area of responsibility covers a third of the country.

John is in the first stages of the planned re-organisation. The revolutionary change is a matter of months away and he is anxiously trying to get the message across to a demotivated and cynical audience that change can be good for them.

'The aim of the changes is to improve service to customers (even though our customers are captive); to demonstrate that we do actually care for our staff; and deliver better value for money by increasing our effectiveness.

'We are now going through the process of selecting area directors – the key people in making it happen. The new managers will have to make their own bids for resources with a small support staff. They will be more independent, and on their own to a far greater degree than ever before. It is a difficult transition for one or two of them to come to terms with. They won't just be able to sit back and do what their predecessors did.

'I have to ensure that managers are empowered to do all that they say they want to do in terms of hiring, firing and budgeting without artificial constraints.

'We expect there will be a lot more give and take and rather less of the barony of the old organisation. But we will still be there sorting out resource management and other issues within our own territories. We will also be looking to make a contribution to central policy, ensuring at board level there is a good appreciation of the concerns in the field.

'The key is to make sure we have proper two-way communications. In the past, it was possible for the policy people to be dislocated from the people putting things into practice.

'You can't ignore the fact that this is a politically sensitive operation. I think we will be in a much better position to say to the central policy-makers, "You want us to do this because there is a political imperative, but remember we agreed these targets at the beginning of the year. Something will have to give. Either the targets will have to give a little bit or we will have to be given resources to complete the task." Recognising our training and other commitments we will know our organisation better as the result of these changes and will be able to deal with political changes of course.

'The new organisation will bring greater clarity so we can operate more effectively upwards – to ministers – and downwards – to our staff. The perception and self-esteem of the staff has been relatively low and that doesn't help in improving our service to the public. We want our staff to see that we are all in the same business and they have proper opportunities to contribute to the formulation of operational policy.

'Having said that, if you ask someone from one of our counters dealing with people what they are in business for they will say to serve the needs of the public. It's quite clear to them. But, as you go up the organisation it becomes rather more diffuse. What we have to do is try to convince people throughout the organisation that serving the public is the purpose of their business as well.

'The problem in my territory is that there is still a lot of regional identity. Part of this is that some areas are regarded as problems and there is a suspicion that, as the new person in charge, I don't really care about them. I have to make the people in those places feel a part of the team.

'I think it's a question of my getting out and about and speaking with managers about the changes we want to see happening. I have to convince them that this is real, happening and we are going to go through with it.

'People have tended to bury their heads in the sand. Some of the people in the local offices think that long-term thinking means next Friday! Others hope that the plans will simply disappear.

'So we need to create cohesion, import some of the better central ideas, like two-way communications, and I have to keep people up to speed with the changes and get them to contribute to the formulation of future policies.

'What I can't afford is for local managers to stand up in front of their key people saying I don't agree with any of this, but it has been decided that this is what has to be done. I have to persuade them to embrace the changes.

'If it works the territory will have a focus and be able to plan its own shape and destiny. We will also be testing the attitude of key players to see if they feel part of the new territory. If they do, they should have brought staff along with them. It is something I want to test personally by talking to managers. It is an important part of my job – spreading the message and listening to what people have to say. The bottom line is how the changes make a difference to someone working in a local office. They have to recognise that the big ideas affect the way they treat the public and give them an opportunity to express their ideas and for them to be listened to.

'In terms of adding value, my role is to provide a clear message and clarify who is responsible for what, so the changes can be introduced speedily and effectively.

'The concern now is how we manage through the changes. It is no good managers talking about a brave new world for the future when you are actually cutting resources. Computerisation has already been decided on. It will save a pre-determined number of staff. The fear is that improvements in efficiency caused by the new computers will be offset by discontent at people losing their jobs. We are highly unionised and, if our service to the public was affected by industrial action, we would be under a lot of political pressure.

'At the first management team meeting we began to grapple with the way in which we are going to put into practice some of the national initiatives we have to progress. The meeting dealt with some immediate issues but was also an important dumping session. People talked about their anxieties and we looked forward to how we are going to structure everything in the future and their role in doing that. It took five hours and was the first meeting of its kind.

'The meeting was held in central London because it was the easiest point of access for all the players. The person who was most inconvenienced was probably me!

'My personal contribution to the meeting was to lead from the front, to deal with personal anxieties about where the managers and their staff stood. I tried to reconcile the differences of view that existed about the way that we might take one section of the business forward. There were a variety of solutions. It was very much about listening, with an eye to feeding some of their concerrns upwards if I thought it is important enough to influence future decision-making.

'Recruiting the new managers is very valuable. I know most of the applicants. They said some very useful things – some positive, some negative – about the way we are trying to shake down the entire organisation. The more positive said "it is important that you choose your managers, it strengthens positions". The more negative said "we are being asked to apply for our own jobs, how can you alienate your most senior level of management?"

'The process of interviewing made it clear that this is for real, we really do mean to make selection competitive – this is clearly a great change from the way the civil service did things in the past. The form of the interviews – very open – also relays a clear message. The process shows jobs are open to competition, not cosy career development moves with people coming from headquarters to manage our units. This has led to a few disagreements with the personnel group at headquarters – it is highly delicate as, to a large extent, my career depends on not upsetting certain of the senior, powerful people in the organisation. I have to convince them and take them with us as well.

'To help me avoid the paperwork that all this is producing I have recruited an assistant. My judgement of him is that he is someone who is good at and flexible with paperwork, good at resource management and interpersonal skills. I need someone to cut through the paperwork.

'It is making a lot of difference. It is important to have someone to bounce ideas off. Instead of returning to the office to find a full in-tray, things are being dealt with and being categorised and prioritised.

'I spend a lot of time visiting offices and talking to managers. I was invited to a prestigious meeting with a senior manager but, along with my colleagues, we just didn't see it as a valuable use of our time. We didn't want to sit around talking vaguely about the next few years. I think this is an interesting change in our outlook. We want to concentrate on our business, getting through the next two or three years and changing things.

'With the area directors in place we plan to gather them for a meeting to map out the timetable for the changes, cover the aims and objectives of the re-organisation and where we expect to be in the first year, as well as the nitty gritty of what we could make different about the first day.

'I think there is a feeling of enthusiasm for the new structure. The managers take the view that they are living in a continuing, uncontrollable climate dictated by headquarters.

'As part of my hearts and minds campaign I went to speak to a meeting of more promising staff at a training event. The joy of this was that it gave me an opportunity to speak to them about what the future was going to be like. The hardest question I was asked was, "How can you prove to us now that life is going to be so much better for the staff in local offices given all the changes that we've got to go through?" It was hard because I knew, to a large extent, they would have to take my word for it. There was nothing concrete they could take away with them; I could give them the vision but not the certainty. The uncertainty, I now realise, goes up and down the organisation.

'In another initiative I set up a number of small working groups on various issues and topics. These fast-reporting, relatively free-thinking groups, send a clear signal that the style of management is changing. The groups are also tackling some of the sacred cows of the organisation. The personnel department, for example, has developed a very complex appraisal system which no one likes. The groups make it clear that we have the authority to develop our own system and abandon the one managers feel was foisted upon them.

'At the moment I doubt whether people at the bottom of the organisation have noticed much difference. In some ways I am not sure we have made as much progress as I anticipated. I don't know if my perceptions of the process have changed – it is difficult to stand back – but it is now a lot more about looking to and contributing to the future. The recruitment process has proved crucial – people are waking up to the fact that these are new jobs and, hopefully, this will be a new organisation.'

Key points

Recruitment

The process of interviewing and appointing people to new jobs has been a major drain on John's time. He uses it as a means of making sure he finds people who support the changes and of making the message clear that changes are real and are happening already. This, of course, runs the risk of selecting people on attitude rather than ability.

Adding value

John feels that he has added an important channel of communication between headquarters and the field. He argues that a focal point is necessary in times of change and that because he has previously done a field job he can help his managers relate the old approach to the new one. He sees his role as providing a supportive focus. This may be similar to providing support for strategy that is being crafted. He says that he occasionally needs to lead from the front but that is not the only way he is operating. He appears to be able to be flexible in his leadership styles and have the necessary interpersonal skills to support in the background and lead dramatically from the front.

Empowering

John is intent on delegating as much as possible. He is also able to give very clear examples of what that process will achieve. He is at his happiest when he has targets and clarity. It seems to be an important part of his personal approach to his job.

His belief in empowerment is such that he also accepts that one possible outcome of the new structure is that he might make himself redundant once the new structure is established.

Commitment

John decided earlier in his career that he didn't want to spend his life preparing defensive documents for ministers. He does not regard himself as an administrator, but as someone who likes to stand up and be counted. He sees his current job as his first real opportunity truly to influence the course of events. Clearly a lot of personal energy and emotion is tied up in this present job.

The personal touch

One of the things that always happens in major change is that people cry out for individual contact. John has great skills in talking to people and conveying messages and listening. He is recognised for this skill, but it brings with it a danger. The danger from above is that people then send you into unreasonably difficult situations. They have an unrealistic expectation about what you can do. The danger from below is that people may perceive you have a strength that they can't match. They may complain that you are very good at persuasion, but that was not what they wanted to talk about. It is a kind of frustration. Though John's colleagues all describe him as a great communicator, the critical issue for him is knowing when to use which style of communication.

References

1. D Quinn Mills, *Rebirth of the Corporation*, John Wiley, 1993.
2. Patricia Scott, 'Living up to expectations' *The Times*, 20 May 1993.
3. Sir Simon Hornby, 'Setting the tone for WH Smith' *Marketing Business*, December 1989.
4. Jean-Louis Barsoux, 'Living up to expectations' *The Times*, 20 May 1993.
5. Jean-Louis Barsoux, 'Living up to expectations' *The Times*, 20 May 1993.

2

FOUNDATIONS FOR HIGH PERFORMANCE

The key characteristics of the high performers. What is it in their behaviour and managerial style which differentiates them from colleagues and competitors?

Managers: unique and individual
Despite formulae for success and generic management education there is no identikit manager.

Recognising and benefitting from your imperfections
Successful they might be, but high performers have a keen awareness of their own limitations and fallibility.

Knowing what you want and achieving it
Clear goals, evolving visions and constant action to achieve them.

Channelling energy and creating commitment
Apparently inexhaustible, high performers display huge reservoirs of commitment.

Using the organisation like a fish in water
Negotiating the maze of corporate machinations, high performers find clear passages, continually at ease with their environment.

Contributing as leader
Not isolated or in the straitjacket of hierarchy, high performers are part of the team.

Key simplicities
Elusive, but omnipresent, these are the personal skills which help high performers.

MANAGERS: UNIQUE AND INDIVIDUAL

The managers we studied were from a variety of businesses and held different positions within their organisations. Perhaps the least surprising conclusion to emerge was that each manager was different in style and method.

There is nothing earth-shattering in this. You would expect the marketing director of a multinational chemical company to have a different approach from the managing director of a small software company. But, it emphasises that solutions to corporate and managerial problems must include some sort of recognition of the individual nature of managers and of the individualistic character of management.

The degree of variance between the behaviour of the high performers was enormous. The differences in behaviour covered the most basic of activities. Something as apparently basic as a daily action plan was handled differently by each of the managers. One said he had four levels of action plan, ranging from what he called 'fly shit', which was written on post-it notes and hardly touched his desk before moving on, through two levels of 'to do' list, to statements on the company strategy which were kept in a folder. Catrina Carlberg kept her diary free for the forthcoming weeks so she could trouble-shoot throughout Europe and be driven by events rather than predetermined plans.

It is not surprising that such everyday activities are handled in different ways. The corollary of this, however, is that if mundane tasks elicit a huge range of responses, criticial strategic and long-term activities are liable to produce an even greater range of techniques, skills and behaviour.

RECOGNISING AND BENEFITING FROM YOUR IMPERFECTIONS

The managers we interviewed were – and are – by most criteria, successful. Yet, success did not appear to have made them entirely sure of themselves. Indeed, they were acutely aware of their own fallibility. What they said was not enshrined as truth in tablets of stone. They had areas of incompetence and were generally aware of them.

Civil servant, John Michaels, commenting on the appointment of his assistant said: 'My judgement of him is that he has the ability to be quick and flexible and is good at resource management and interpersonal skills.' The manager did not make statements about reality, but about his interpretation of it. He was able to cope with other people's opinions and judgements however different they might be from his own.

Again, this is not altogether surprising. But, it does run counter to a lot of the macho-management championed in the 1980s where admissions of fallibility and failure were few and far between.

It is, to a large extent, a matter of honesty. It is something which Robert Haas, chairman and chief executive of Levi Strauss, has argued strongly for throughout his time at the company. Describing his company's approach, he says:

> *Senior managers try to be explicit about our vulnerability and failings. We talk to people about the bad decisions we've made. It de-mystifies senior management and removes the stigma traditionally associated with taking risks. We also talk about the limitations of our own knowledge, mostly by inviting other people's perspectives.*[1]

The high performers were also prepared to accept that an imperfectly formed idea might well crystallise into something useful if they talked about it with someone else. This runs against the behaviour of many managers who demand certainty in an increasingly uncertain environment. 'People just don't say they have a hazy idea and they want to talk about it,' said one manager. 'That's not manly enough for them.'

Such attitudes have important repercussions for learning within the organisation (which is discussed later). They also undercut any chance of managerial adulation. Managers are human too, and the good ones have recognised that fundamental truism.

And yet, admitting to fallibility and imperfection is not necessarily an easy process. One manager we talked to was a director of a small engineering company. Over a period of a few years he began to lose faith in some of the decisions of the company's chief executive. Though he was deeply unhappy with the direction the company was being taken, he remained silent. The chief executive was a personal friend so he didn't want to sour their relationship. He convinced himself that the fault lay with him – he didn't understand or was not equipped to deliver what the chief executive wanted.

He could not face up to the fact that his reactions were normal and the sensible thing to do would be to explain his reservations and concerns to the chief executive. To assuage his guilt and unease, he began to work longer hours. This led to ever increasing frustration.

After two years he came out and admitted his concerns. By then it was too late – the chief executive was confused by his years of silence and the diligent hours which seemed to demonstrate commitment. Their friendship ended and the director moved to another company where his commitment is expressed in a genuine belief in what he is doing rather than by spending hours at his desk.

KNOWING WHAT YOU WANT AND ACHIEVING IT

'You read a book from beginning to end. You run a business the opposite way. You start with the end, and do everything you must to reach it,' observed the legendary boss of ITT, Harold Geneen.[2]

'We didn't argue what the computer should be, we all knew what the computer should be. Our job was to go out and make it work,' commented one of the design engineers on the Apple Mackintosh team.[3]

Such clarity of purpose is rare – for all the mission statements and visionary exhortations by executives in annual reports.

Peter Drucker cut to the heart of the problem in a comparison of Japanese and Western attitudes. 'One of the greatest differences between the Japanese and Europeans and Americans is that they don't take their mission for granted. They start off with "What are we trying to do?" Not, "How do we do it?" '[4]

For the high performers, clarity and action were continually emphasised. They seldom use the language of strategy or leadership – or even the words themselves. The word 'vision' was used occasionally but, for the most part, they want to talk about what they did and what they plan to do. Simple 'doing' words were their most common vocabulary.

This is combined with intense clarity of purpose. Although all of the subjects had deliberately chosen to discuss issues where they had not formed a clear plan, they all showed great certainty in establishing their purpose. Even though they didn't know how they were going to achieve the goal, there was no doubt that they wanted to reach it and would know when they had achieved their objectives.

There are two central paradoxes in this philosophy. Vision has, like many other aspects of management, become a corporate rather than a personal thing. In our study these successful managers channelled their personal vision into the corporate vision so that the two merged and integrated. The second paradox lies in the flexibility of their approach. The high performers did not accept vision as a settled or static concept.

Vision: living and mobile

Having a mobile, yet clear and committed vision is critical in achieving high performance. It unites and enables different teams, departments and individuals to forget their differences and work towards a strong, common goal. It is not a public relations exercise or a derided mission statement pinned on factory notice boards. It is a real and living *raison d'être*.

The visions of the managers were not the type you usually find faithfully recorded in annual reports. They were more unstructured, but were still the driving force behind many, if not all, their activities. They had some long-term notion of how they were adding value to a particular project or to their organisation as a whole.

The mobility of their visions was striking. In fact, they appeared to have no idea of a fixed vision. When asked about the future, their vision of each stage – whether it is six months, a year, two years, five years or ten years – differed considerably. The visions of these high performers were continually developing, altering and being enhanced.

In practice this means that their visions have practical value. When things go wrong they are able to be philosophical. A setback does not render their vision worthless. Instead, it means that the vision has to be achieved in a slightly different way.

In contrast, many organisations appear to treat corporate visions as disposable items. When the going gets tough visions are jettisoned with apparent impunity as concern with the next crisis fills managerial minds. Announcing an $8.9 billion pre-tax restructuring charge to cover job losses and plant cut backs, IBM chairman and chief executive, Lou Gerstner, commented:

> *There has been a lot of speculation that I'm going to deliver a 'vision' of [the future of] IBM. The last thing IBM needs right now is a vision. What IBM needs right now is a series of very tough-minded, market-driven [and] highly effective strategies that deliver performance in the market place and shareholder value.*[5]

Gerstner's comments suggest that any vision of the future had been sacrificed to short-term expediency; if IBM could get out of the mire, the future would shape itself.

For the high performers the way their visions are moving provides a constant reference point for their day-to-day actions. They are like characters in a novel who are gradually shaping the plot and developing their own personalities as they progress towards a finale, undefined in the author's head but increasingly clear in those of the characters.

Karl-Heinz Muller has a vision of how the project he is

managing should progress and end up. 'You start with an ideal of how the project is to be executed,' he says. As the project progresses his expectations change and develop. His role in achieving this was to dive in and solve problems where he sees them. He is able to be objective, despite the demanding nature of the project. But, more importantly, he realises the project could survive almost as easily without him.

Catrina Carlberg has a similar approach. She deals with things that other people have failed to pick up on and is able to pinpoint potential problem areas.

Central to their vision is a keen awareness of their own role. They are like plumbers who mysteriously know the exact place to hit a troublesome boiler. Their ability to learn, perceive, influence and alter, continually adds value to the organisation.

CHANNELLING ENERGY AND CREATING COMMITMENT

Most of the autobiographies of the great and the good in the corporate world, reveal individuals with enormous reservoirs of energy. To a large extent it is still expected that successful managers work their colleagues to a standstill.

On the surface, there is a lot of misplaced machismo at work. The boss stays longer at the office to prove he or she has something extra, the invincibility of authority.

It is easy to be cynical about such an approach. There is – especially among the English – a tendency to deride such commitment and celebrate the amateur. Obsessional professionals are often derided as blinkered and narrow.

Among the managers, there was tremendous drive and

energy to find effective ways of achieving their goals, once they had convinced themselves they were important. Even though they sometimes had to face considerable opposition, the managers didn't waiver.

It is not simply a matter of putting more hours in than their colleagues. Though some, like Karl-Heinz Muller, certainly do that. Their examples go further. John Michaels, for example, arranges to bring managers together from throughout the country. The location he chooses is the one most inconvenient to him – the message to the others is that the subject is important enough for him to make a sacrifice.

Ken Lawrie recounts how, at an important strategy meeting, a lengthy discussion narrowed things down to five options. While his management team went away for an evening's relaxation, he wrote a summary of each of the five options. Next morning, when the meeting re-started, the options were before each of the managers.

Clearly, the high performers expend a lot of energy and effort in their work. They are highly committed, but not blindly so. But, there is a balance to their activities. Work is important certainly but, in the final analysis, not vitally so.

USING THE ORGANISATION LIKE A FISH IN WATER

Aquariums are commonly believed to be therapeutic. No doubt there are senior managers who relieve the excesses of stress by staring at their guppies and tetras. For the manager, besieged by calls, meetings and the need for instant decisions, the attraction is simple – the colourful fish are effortlessly in control. It is a state which managers find difficult to achieve at any point in their careers.

Management theorist Warren Bennis temporarily gave up theorising in the 1970s to become president of the University of Cincinnati with 70,000 students and 2,600 faculty. He recalls the discontent he felt as he looked out of the window to see the gardener cutting the grass. 'As a supposed leader, I watch with envy the superior autonomy of the man mowing the university lawn, in complete control of the machine he rides, the total arbiter on which swath to cut, where and when. I cannot match it.'[6] Bennis soon left the job, his theories having been disappointed by reality.

As any gardener will tell you, it is simplistic and patronising to suggest that there is no stress or worry attached to cultivating healthy lawns, but it was notable among the managers we studied that they all were very integrated into their surroundings. Not for them the romantic view of the autonomous world of the gardener. They took it for granted that they could move through the organisation easily and swiftly. Achieving agreement from people, getting clearance for projects, were minor hindrances rather than weighty obstacles to reaching their goals.

The process of moving through and utilising the resources of their organisation was often an unconscious one. The managers did it so well they often didn't realise that was what they were doing. It is akin to a hurdler reaching his or her peak – automatically they take the right number of strides between hurdles. They don't need to think or alter their stride pattern. It is natural and effective.

Ken Lawrie explained how he managed to negotiate the corporate maze to ensure the new strategic plan was accepted:

I spent time talking to everyone about the implications of the strategy. I didn't want it to be an enormous shock to them, but for them to feel part of the process. Once a week, I talked to most of the people who run the company, using the 'phone a lot . . . and travelling a great deal to maintain more informal conversations. I find it useful to travel with people so they have the opportunity to talk. I also get my secretary to button-hole key people. This is a crucial part of getting ownership and influence.

Moving easily through the organisation, Ken has no problem in arranging meetings and bringing the right people together. While he recognises that this is one of his core skills, he also acknowledges that others are not so accomplised in extracting what they want from the organisation.

Among the high performers, Karl-Heinz Muller was a very good example of a manager who was working within an apparently complex system yet was able to keep things as simple as possible. His central problem was a logistical one – quite simply he was usually in the wrong continent. He had to respond if there was a problem at the chemical plant in South America even if he was in Germany or elsewhere. Key to his approach was his ability to extract clear data from the organisation by asking the right questions at the right level.

This sort of situation is now commonplace. While once management was a very immediate activity with problems in front of you and the protagonists probably there also, now managers have to cope with being at a distance from events. Instead of being daunted – as many would be – by the inadequacies of the South American 'phone system and other such logistical nightmares, Karl-Heinz was uniformly calm, seeking out positive opportunities in the system rather than being overwhelmed.

Multinational executive David Andrews knew that his boss had failed to achieve what David intended to do. Even so, he had a high degree of faith in his ability to cut through organisational lethargy.

> *We identified a focal person in each section who would be responsible for collecting all the data. We had a kind of underground network of people . . . My technique was to use people whom I knew were owed some favours by many of the units and get them to call some of those favours in.*

This gave the international managers the impression that the process was something they could contribute to and gain from, rather than yet another edict from the distant headquarters.

By talking to people, approaching allies in the right way at the right time, knowing how the system works, the high performers are able to eradicate a great deal of delaying bureaucracy and corporate politics to concentrate on action. Within their organisations they behave as fish in water but, in addition, are acutely aware of which environment – which waters – they operate most effectively in.

CONTRIBUTING AS LEADER

There is the temptation to categorise leadership into two distinct approaches, at the opposite end of a spectrum. In the first, the leader is all-dominant, deciding everything and implementing most of the decisions personally. At the oppposite extreme there is the leader who delegates so successfully that he or she appears blithely unaware of the reality of implementation.

The middle ground between dictatorship and distance is more elusive. Despite being at or near the top of the organisation, high performance managers wanted to contribute directly to the process of implementation. They wanted to be seen as resources rather than distant despots or continual sources of interference. Not content with being leaders, high performers wanted to contribute as individuals.

Ken Lawrie set up a major project group to produce a report of strategic needs and data for the organisation. He made the most junior member of his team chair the meetings although he himself attended. Of course everyone knew Ken was the boss, but Ken felt more able to contribute than if he had been chairing the meetings. His estimate was that he contributed for about 30 per cent of the time.

Most of the other managers shared a similar belief in allowing others to have their say and contributing rather than dominating or dictating. While the textbooks advocate teamwork, they are team players by instinct.

KEY SIMPLICITIES

After tracking the managers for some time, Karl-Heinz Muller was discussing the huge and very complex project he was involved in managing. He had previously shown us the enormously detailed and lengthy reports that were produced every month charting each aspect of the work. The quantity of the data was vast; too much for one person to keep on top of. The number of possible interactions caused by a single component being delayed, another needing to be re-designed and a third needing substitute materials was astronomical. There seemed a high probability of something going wrong and not being noticed until it was too late.

'How do you develop a sixth sense to warn you if something is going wrong? How can you tell when you have so much data to digest?' Karl-Heinz paused, and seemed to lower his voice on the 'phone. You could almost imagine him looking over his shoulder to ensure that no one else was listening. He replies,

> *If I think something is not quite right I ask for a small report on that specific area. The trouble is that I might be in Germany rather than on site when I see something in our monthly report which concerns me . . . Often you can't be face-to-face with people on site. Talking by telephone is complicated by the South American 'phone system and the time difference. What we do is send short faxes. If I write down a problem it becomes clearer. The same applies to my people – if they have a problem they write it down and send it to me. The engineers are usually working on other projects so they don't have much time.*

Quick and handwritten in German, these small reports alerted Karl-Heinz to potential trouble spots. In effect, they cut through the complexity of the project.

It was undoubtedly a good technique, and one that other project managers could learn from. But there was something about the way Karl-Heinz had talked about it, that suggested it was something more than a casual technique. He seemed reticent, almost shy, about revealing this information. It was as if it was a secret and he was telling us about it as a personal favour. Certainly he had incorporated the technique into his personal style.

Karl-Heinz's tone was reminiscent of the way a child will show you something that is precious, even if it is just a piece of wood found on the beach. Strangely, several of the other managers had used a similar tone of voice when explaining how they go about making sure things are done. Ken Lawrie said that he often tried to travel with his managers, even though he personally preferred travelling alone. Why? 'Because you can talk with people on a long plane journey in a way that doesn't happen at meetings.'

Looking back over the transcripts and notes, several more of these slightly idiosyncratic, apparently unimportant, techniques came to light. 'When dealing with a problem I tend to make notes of pluses and minuses and possible action and that sort of thing,' said the sales director of one company. 'I find that when I do this I can prompt myself very well. I weigh up things, put in pluses and minuses on bits of paper and then try to form a decision from them.'

Jotting things down appeared to act as an important aid to his thinking processes. For this manager, all actions had a set of positive and negative implications – he was not, however, afraid of acknowledging and confronting the negatives. It is straightforward – again almost childlike – but this manager found it re-assuring and helpful. Not only that, most people have probably followed a similar approach at some time or another, but he had thought about it, used it and *recognised* how it worked for him.

In the high-technology age, sitting down with a scrap of paper was extremely popular, perhaps re-assuring. 'I sit down with a piece of paper and work out all the things I need to do and what I have done so far. As I do it, I can feel it getting easier,' one of the managers said.

Again it seems obvious. But, in fact, the manager took the time to put things down in this particular way. Besieged by calls and deadlines, this simple approach was attractively objective and isolated from the maelstrom of other pressing activities.

Other managers have similarly idiosyncratic approaches to apparently simple things. They all enabled them to do their jobs better. We were surprised to find that Catrina Carlberg's diary was not booked up more than a week ahead. She realises that the crucial demand on her time – the needs of customers – was difficult to forecast. In a single week she found time to spend a day at her office in Stockholm; visit suppliers in Norway; sign a contract in Holland; travel to Lapland to meet customers and attend a banquet for the Swedish royal family. None of these events had been planned more than a few days in advance.

For Catrina the freedom created by not being tied down to meetings and timings was a central part of her management technique. People inside and outside the company knew that if she was needed at a particular place, she would almost certainly be there.

We have labelled such techniques as *key simplicities*.

The key simplicities are a means of by-passing managerial inertia. They enable and facilitate action. They are a means by which managers process and communicate information; how they make sense of complexity.

Though key simplicities are very individualistic, there was one which was common to several of the managers: they much preferred to go and see managers in their own locations rather than call them up to head office. Ken Lawrie had made a return trip to South America in 48 hours primarily to visit one manager. It happened that this manager came to Europe quite frequently and it would have been possible to arrange to meet him during the next trip. Was it an unnecessary use of resources? Ken was sure it was a good idea. 'Our meeting will be better if I am on his territory,' he explained with forceful simplicity.

Apparently straightforward, the advantages of the key simplicities are highly significant (see Table 2.1). Repeated

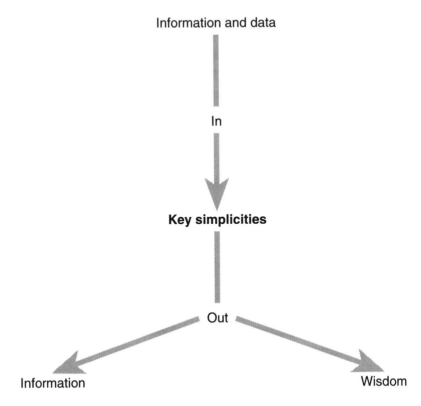

Figure 2.1 Key simplicities

as anecdotes, or as hints and tips for being a better manager, key simplicities do not seem immediately to hold any great significance. However, talking to groups of managers about key simplicities quickly leads to them admitting to their own. Most managers seem to rely on no more than four. And they are not just techniques.

A key simplicity seems to embody some kind of value or belief. So when the person is using it, he or she is operating in a way that to them is right. It seems to fit in with their personal values. The use of the simplicity is a positive reinforcement of their management style and thinking.

Table 2.1 The advantages of the key simplicities

Key simplicity	Achievement
Short reports	Problem spotting
	Problem solving
	Clear communications
	Efficient monitoring
Travelling with colleages	Clear communications
	Sounding board for ideas
	Learning from others
	Encouraging openness
Jotting down pros and cons	Simplifying complex issues
	Making time to think
	Problem solving
Keeping diary free	Making time for customers and employees
	Problem solving
	Flexibility
	Speed of response
Face-to-face contact	Breaking barriers
	Clear communications
	Building trust
	Developing relationships

Even so, the key simplicities are not an antidote to all known managerial ills. They can work negatively.

One manager we talked to had risen rapidly in a highly political organisation. After a series of promotions he was turned down for a more senior job. Initially he blamed himself and the political manoeuvres of his colleagues. As he looked more closely at his approach, however, he realised that his key simplicity was an ability to see the best of everything. At every turn, no matter what had happened, he made the past look good. If there was an error or oversight he managed to play down his role in it, to emerge with his reputation unblemished and usually enhanced.

His key simplicity had, up to a point, worked successfully for him. It meant, however, that he was unable to identify where he had made rash predictions, crass errors or simply failed to live up to his own hyperbole. In effect, the key simplicity hastened his career advancement, but blocked opportunities for learning along the way. He emerged politically sophisticated and highly disenchanted. As a first stage in his development he learned to admit to his failures, acknowledge his limitations and come to terms with his potentially helpful key simplicity.

Even though the high performers are operating in a complex and ambiguous world, the key simplicity brings some clarity to what they are doing, because it is simple but not simplistic. It is like a personal magic carpet on which the high performers are more likely to produce successful results.

Because each manager has developed the method for him or herself, and has not consciously learned it from someone else, they use it instinctively. They don't engage in time-consuming logical analysis, it is naturally integrated into their way of working and therefore feels easy. Finally, and perhaps more important, the high performers know that key simplicities work. They are intuitively aware of their capabilities, so that when they recognise that they can be utilised, then in some way the outcome is more likely to be guaranteed.

References

1. Robert Haas, 'Values Make the Company' *Harvard Business Review*, September/October 1990.
2. Harold Greneen, quoted in *Makers of Management*, David Clutterbuck and

Stuart Crainer, Macmillan, 1990.
3. Apple Mackintosh, quoted in 'Enhancing Strategic Thought', Phil Hodgson, unpublished paper, 1991.
4. Peter Drucker, quoted in *Makers of Management*, David Clutterbuck and Stuart Crainer, Macmillan 1990.
5. Lou Gerstner, 'Gerstner sees no place for a vision at IBM', *Financial Times*, 28 July 1993.
6. Warren Bennis, 'Doing the right thing', *The Director*, October 1988.

3

HIGH PERFORMANCE BUILDING BLOCKS

**High performance makes strategy happen.
Analysis of traditional and new approaches to
converting good ideas into implementation.**

Why strategy is more than a game of chess
Is corporate strategy simply a question of knowing the rules and becoming a grandmaster, or more to do with possibilities than solutions?

The route to strategic inertia
Despite the best intentions, strategy too often restricts and inhibits rather than releases ideas.

Transforming analysis to action
A vicious circle has developed with strategy perpetually stalled by the demand for more and more analysis.

The failure of management by objectives
With goals moving continually, the direct route from A to B is no longer clear.

Moving beyond the magic formula for success
The short life of the mythical quick-fix.

Creating certainty from chaos
If managers no longer have total control over things strategic, what is their new role?

Strategy that works
The linear route from idea to implementation no longer works, so how can managers beat the strategic gridlock?

WHY STRATEGY IS MORE THAN A GAME OF CHESS

As a manager, John Charles is intuitive, sometimes agg-ressively so, coming up with off-beat ideas which he enthusiastically seeks to understand and communicate. He is also an excellent chess player. By using comparisons with chess he tries to clear his mind of the detritus which surrounds decision-making. He envisages a game of clear rules, where there is a winner and a loser, and all possible moves can be anticipated. Yet, paradoxically, the metaphor allows him to accept that, within the framework of the rules, there is room for intuitive decisions – moves that defy conventional logic.

In chess there are two extreme schools of thought. The first says that it is a scientific game and, if you built a computer it would play chess better than any human. It would analyse all the positions and combinations. The second approach says that individuals don't analyse each line. It is not a game for computers. Sometimes we make sacrifices – we make a move because it looks and feels right. That's how people play – and that's how I manage. It is partly based on the experience of being in similar positions before. You remember what you did and if it worked. But it is also the fact that you can't analyse the situation completely. It feels right, you work down the path, you begin to see where it is leading you and then you go there.

The traditional approach to strategy has sought to create the managerial equivalent of the computer grandmaster. A manager who *knows* all the moves should always be able to make the right moves. Although even grandmasters lose games, intuitive and individualistic approaches, such as John's, have tended to be overlooked.

This approach – putting faith in accumulating knowledge of all the moves possible – has had a crucial effect on management education which has tended to concentrate on adding new moves to managers' armouries, rather than giving them a broader awareness of the game they are playing.

Despite the apparent certainty of his chess metaphor, John Charles's management style is characterised by pragmatism. In an ideal world, he recognises that management would be like playing computer-generated chess: strategy would and could be developed to take into account every eventuality, every move the opposition may make. He realises that this is not the case, but still retains his faith in the chess analogy. He believes that by continuing to experience different managerial situations and learning from them, his skills will continually develop. He will never reach the status of computer grandmaster, but aspiring to that level – accepting possibilities and fallibilities – is John's fundamental managerial mission.

THE ROUTE TO STRATEGIC INERTIA

At the other extreme from John, is a strategic planning manager from a multinational corporation. To carry on John's metaphor, the planning manager spends his time creating grandmaster standard strategies – the trouble is that the people in the organisation are rank amateurs with little knowledge, expertise or interest in the game. There is a massive mismatch between the strategies he creates and implementation. Sitting in an office high above the City of London, he talked about his company's strategic plan for the forthcoming financial year. The plan covers half of the company. Many hundreds of man-hours have been invested in developing the plan which now stretches to thirty pages. It is on his desk, marked 'Strictly Confidential'.

There isn't really a theme to the plan. It fits in with our overall business objectives, our mission. Hardly anyone actually gets to see the finished article, just my boss and four or five others – the people who really drive the business.

He is uncomfortable with the futility of his work. Directionless and unread except by a coterie of senior executives, the strategic plan is blissfully unconnected to the real world. Sales people will never see it or even be aware of it. Managers may mention the document in hushed tones, but will not be allowed to analyse it or come up with their own ideas on how it could be improved. Yet, this document is the guiding light behind the way the company performs and goes about its business for the following twelve months.

Such strategic planning is patently worthless. It is built around the fear of failure. If people know of the clearly defined performance objectives, how will they react if targets are not reached? How will they regard the managers who set the unachievable figures? What if they disagree with the objectives and no longer wish to belong to the company? Fear stalks the closely typed pages and flow charts of such plans as surely as it dominates the process behind it.

Though the example is an extreme one, it is true and an all too frequent occurrence. While the development of strategic thought, and in particular strategic analysis, has been considerable in recent years, managers and organisations are still faced with the problem of converting strategy into action.

Nowhere is this more evident than in change management.

A survey of top executives in 250 UK companies by KPMG Management Consulting found that only 31 per cent believed their change programmes were 'very effective'. 'Identifying the need for change is relatively straightforward for executives, what really causes problems is making change happen successfully,' observes the KPMG survey.[1]

Implementation is often assumed. Strategy is handed down without explanation. Such assumptions are not solely the preserve of strategists. Managers often believe that simple decisions are automatically implemented.

'There is a tendency to believe that implementation is fairly straightforward. People will tackle things automatically in the same way as they did a similar thing in the past,' observed a management development director. He went on to suggest that, for senior managers, the assumption that good ideas were put into practice was perhaps inevitable – 'Senior managers don't get the benefit of having to sell their ideas. They often get green lights all the way through and believe, therefore, that things get done.'

The truth for many managers is that thinking about problems is the easy bit; implementing strategy is the hard part of their job.

Recent disasters have provided many examples of vacuum-based management, with managers assuming that their decisions are put into practice by those lower down the corporate hierarchy. Before a major rail disaster, managers laid down guidelines on how engineers should go about re-wiring operations. Having produced the guidelines, management did not check that engineers actually did what they were asked to do. They didn't. Under pressure and tired from overwork, engineers took shortcuts which eventually led to tragic loss of life.

The capsize of the Townsend Thoresen ferry *Herald of Free Enterprise* produced another example of managers distanced from reality. Standing orders for the ferry, drawn up by managers, ignored changes in manning levels and, as a result, key personnel were expected to be in two places at once. Basic operations were inadequately monitored. One such operation was overlooked and led to the loss of 193 lives.

During the inquiry into the *Piper Alpha* oil rig disaster, the union representative argued that the gulf between management and what actually went on was similarly broad. He said: 'The whole management evidence from Occidental [the owners of the rig] paints a picture of complete ignorance of the problems which existed. The senior management provided no suport to the platform staff. They provided no training. They provided no guidance. They laid down no procedures. They did not participate in discussions with the operators. They did not seek the views of their employees'.[2]

Similar problems afflict strategic management. There has developed what could be called a strategy gap, a gaping chasm between strategy and action. Strategy carefully crafted and supported by analysis, too often fails to be converted into action. That implementation is one of the biggest obstacles to effective management at a senior level should come as no surprise. The considerable emphasis on leadership in the last few years is in recognition of the fact that implementation often requires more skills than those which created the plan in the first place.

Managing chaos, coping with paradox, in fact all of the work on managing change, demonstrates that managers are aware that the demands of their jobs are changing. Having taken this first step of recognition, however, managers are then faced with the sometimes distressing realisation that they too must change.

Part of the problem is that some managers are unable to watch strategy happening. Having come up with a bright idea, they tinker and interfere as it is implemented. They don't want to let go. Part of the reason for this is that managers tend to be a little uncomfortable with the concept of others doing the dirty work. They want to join in.

'Managers often only get respect by involving themselves in the system. Managers spend time proving they can use a screwdriver and are better at adding up than the accountant,' observed the management development director. Managers, it seems, are still not equipped with the necessary skills to take a broader view. As a result, they think in terms of short-term tactics. Only later do these add up to a strategy.

TRANSFORMING ANALYSIS TO ACTION

The fuel for the growth in interest in all things strategic has been analysis. While analysis has been the watchword, data has been the password. Managers have assumed that anything which could not be analysed could not be managed. The last thirty years have seen a relentless search for things, actions and decisions which can be analysed. The belief in analysis is part of a relentless search for a logical commercial regime, a system of management which will, under any circumstances, produce a successful result. But effective analysis does not guarantee effective, or even appropriate, implementation.

Igor Ansoff, one of the driving forces behind the development of strategic management, has lamented: 'As firms became increasingly skilful strategy formulators, the translation of strategy into results in the marketplace lagged behind. This created "paralysis by analysis" in strategic planning and suppression of strategic planning in many firms.'[3]

Indeed, all the analysis in the world can lead to decisions which are plainly wrong. IBM had all the data about its markets, yet reached the wrong conclusions. It is a problem not restricted to business. British Prime Minister Harold Macmillan was once asked what was the most difficult thing about his job. 'Events, my dear boy, events,' he replied. For all its usefulness, analysis does not dictate events.

The way managers are conditioned to approach budgets is typical of the thirst for analysis. We talked to Franz, head of a major department in a large European company.

> *I have been working on our budget for next year for six months already. It started in August and finishes in March. On average I probably spend half a day a week on the budget. There are also many meetings.*
>
> *It is, I know, a waste of my time. It becomes pure horse trading. I ask for 20 per cent more than I need. This is slowly cut down. But, if I put in an honest bid for what I need, it would be cut to ribbons. I play the game every year. What else can I do? It is the only way I can make things happen.*

For Franz, budgets and the analysis they involve are a waste of valuble management time. Their relationship to reality, he candidly admits, is zero.

There are many such examples of individual managers who know they can make better use of their time but are constrained by corporate systems and expectations. If Franz failed to produce the figures to back up his budget, he would probably lose his job.

Yet, international management education has been built around the belief that analysis is fundamental to strategic management. It can, after all, be more easily taught than personnel issues which involve such imponderables as human emotions, aspirations and fears. There is also a notable tendency for strategy to be taught by people who come from a numerate background. In contrast, subjects such as leadership tend to be taught by psychologists.

This bias has evolved slowly. Twenty years ago, Harvard ran two strategy courses as part of its MBA programme: one covered analysis, the other implementation. As time progressed, they found it far easier to find material for the analysis course. It was also more straightforward to teach and students preferred it. Gradually the courses became more analytical.

There are two basic problems with the reliance on analysis. First, it is all technique. Watching the implementation of a strategy which is based solely on analysis is like watching a synthesiser recreate the sound of a Stradivarius. It is hollow and de-humanised. Even in this technological age, de-humanised management remains a contradiction in terms.

The second problem goes to the root of the strategy gap. Analysis produces a self-increasing loop. The belief is that more and more analysis will bring safer and safer decisions. If analysis is insufficient, the manager begins to feel guilty. How can they produce a strategy when the data is non-existent or insubstantial? To assuage the guilt they carry out some more analysis. The process continues, relentlessly delaying any decision-making. In such cases, strategy is driven by guilt and fuelled by analysis. Eventually, enough data is bound to filter through and a strategy of sorts will emerge. The process is, however, time-consuming and tortuous. Before the resulting strategy becomes action it is likely that the self-perpetuating combination of analysis and guilt will continue to interfere with and slow the process. Each stage of implementation is

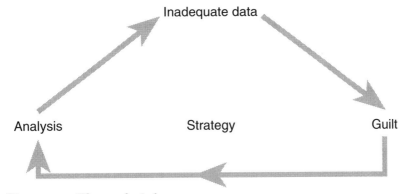

Figure 3.1 The analysis loop

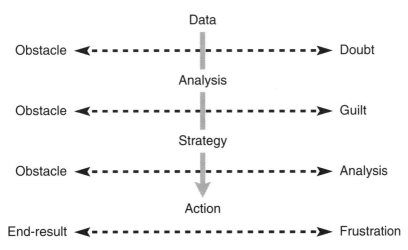

Figure 3.2 The route to frustration, not achievement

likely to be held back by further analysis. The end-result is frustration rather than achievement.

When strategy eventually sees the light of day it is not surprising that the people who are supposed to implement it often shrug their shoulders and carry on as before. Analysis brings strategy into disrepute. Instead of happening, strategy slowly merges into the organisation as if by osmosis.

If strategy is to achieve change, people must believe in the strategy and the necessity for change. A report of analytical data is not usually the most persuasive of documents.

Too often in organisations analysis is used as a defence mechanism rather than as a means of improving individual and corporate performance. Analysis may breed security, but it also inculcates the corporate culture with fearfulness and inertia. Attempts at change merely increase the overall atmosphere.

David Andrews laboured long and hard to create strategy. Along the way he realised that the corporate machine could only take so many new ideas on-board at one time. It was a creature of habits, not all of which were healthy.

In the strategies that had been there a long time we were doing well because they were part of our normal way of doing business. But the relatively new things, that had come up in the last year or two, often had no people committed to them. The strategy was not being fulfilled. There were clear gaps.

Breaching the defensive wall of habitual behaviour was a matter of attrition rather than all-out frontal assault, of incremental change rather than revolution.

Some of the international business world's leading companies have found themselves hidebound by this loop of inaction. Dow Jones, owner of *The Wall Street Journal*, provides one example.

The company's chief executive admitted: 'We're afraid to fail.' In the early 1970s, Dow considered upgrading its dull weekly *Baron's* to a glossy magazine. But it blanched at the risks involved – all the market analysis in the world could not guarantee success. Twenty years on and the publication's circulation remains fixed around its 1970 level. Dow also thought of launching a new business magazine. It got so far as producing a dummy copy, but again it didn't reach the newstands.

In 1981 Dow could have bought electronic information company Telerate for $80 million. It didn't. Instead it slowly built up its share of the business. As it did so, Telerate became hugely successful – the data encouraging further purchases of shares. In 1990 the purchase was eventually completed – for a total of $1.6 billion.

For Dow, avoiding risks, waiting for analysis to come up with foolproof solutions, has proved the riskiest course of all. Corporately, Dow reached a state of inertia. On an individual level, the ramifications are equally great. Instilling independence of mind to take decisions and accept risk is not something which can be achieved overnight. In such an environment it is unlikely to be achieved at all.

In other instances, strategy is carefully drawn up but ignores the human implications of putting it into practice. Analysing human emotions and reactions has never been, and never will be, an exact science. It defies traditional strategic thought.

In one example, a diversified corporation attempted to gain synergy from two of its businesses in totally different fields: water treatment and electronic controls. The strategy was plausible. It aimed to bring life to the low technology water treatment division by developing new electronic controls for its devices. Divisional heads were enthusiastic and helped to develop the strategy but, after several years, the company had to admit failure. Almost no new commercially viable equipment had been developed.

This is how the head of the water treatment division, explains what went wrong:

The problem was not difficult to diagnose. We were used to dealing with government clients where, weighed down with bureaucracy, decisions were made without undue haste. In contrast, the electronic control staff were used to a fast-moving environment with much more sophisticated and demanding customers. We were dealing with tortoises; they were used to hares.

The company's strategy demanded that we co-operated. In practice, it was simply impossible. My people didn't like electronic control laying down exacting delivery dates. Our customers did not take too kindly to the more assertive marketing techniques the company adopted. We couldn't get the best of both worlds. The sacrifices and changes in working attitudes and practices were too large. It looked good on paper and I was as enthusiastic as anyone, but it just didn't take into account the people in the business and how we were used to doing things.

Strategy had ignored the people involved in making it happen.

The truth for senior managers is that strategy no longer exists in isolation. It is increasingly, and has to be, regarded as part of a broader spectrum of managerial skills.

This trend is not, as yet, fully recognised by business schools. Teachers of strategy tend to be from a numerate background. While they tend to talk in digital, leadership tends to be taught by people who talk in poetry.

This divide is glaringly exposed by a simple look at magazine articles. One run through of a database found 17,076 articles on strategy; 2,344 on leadership and a mere forty-nine which mentioned both strategy and leadership. Yet, even the most ardent strategist would be likely to agree that leadership is a key factor in converting strategy into action.

THE FAILURE OF MANAGEMENT BY OBJECTIVES

Under the traditional paradigm, strategy is concerned with making predictions based on analysis. Predictions, and the analysis which forms them, lead to security.

The bottom-line is not expansion, future growth or increased profitability – it is survival. The assumption is that growth and increased profits will naturally follow. If, by using this technique called strategy, we can increase our chances of predicting successful methods, then our successful methods will lead us to survival and perhaps even improvement. So strategy is to do with getting it right or, as the more competitive would say, winning. Of course, it is possible to win battles and lose wars and so strategy has also grown up in the context of linking together a series of actions with some longer-term goals or aims.

In the 1960s predictions and strategies were formed with confidence and optimism. Security could be found. The business environment appeared to be re-assuringly stable. Objectives could be set and strategies developed to meet them in the knowledge that the over-riding objective would not change.

Such an approach, identifying a target and developing strategies to achieve it, became known as 'Management by Objectives' (MBO). Under MBO, strategy formulation was seen as a conscious, rational process. MBO ensured that the plan was carried out. The overall process was heavily logical and, indeed, any other approach (such as an emotional one) was seen as distinctly inappropriate. The thought process was backed with hard data. There was a belief that effective analysis produced a single, right answer; a clear plan was possible and, once it was made explicit, would need to be followed through exactly and precisely.

In practice, the MBO approach demanded too much data. It became overly complex. It also relied too heavily on the past to predict the future. The entire system was ineffective at handling, encouraging or adapting to change. MBO simplified management to a question of reaching A from B using as direct a route as possible (see Figure 3.3). Under MBO, the ends justified the means. The managerial equivalent of motorways were developed in order to reach objectives quickly with the minimum hindrance from outside forces.

'The confusion of means and ends characterises our age,' management guru Henry Mintzberg observed and, today, the motorways are liable to be gridlocked. When the motorways are blocked managers need to use country lanes and B-roads if they are to reach their objectives . . . and then comes the final confusion: the destination is likely to have

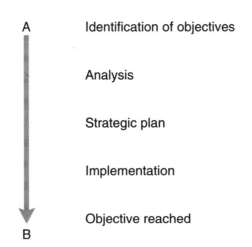

Figure 3.3 The way we were: meeting objectives in the 1960s

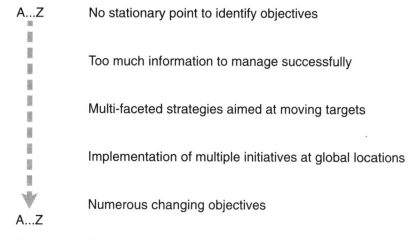

A...Z   No stationary point to identify objectives

               Too much information to manage successfully

               Multi-faceted strategies aimed at moving targets

               Implementation of multiple initiatives at global locations

               Numerous changing objectives
A...Z

Figure 3.4   The way we are: meeting objectives in the 1990s

changed during their journey. The simple A to B route now takes in most of the rest of the alphabet (see Figure 3.4). While MBO sought to narrow objectives and ignore all other forces, success (the objective) is now less easy to identify. Today's measurement of success can include everything from environmental performance to meeting equal opportunities targets. Success has expanded beyond the bottom-line.

As Murray Dalziel, managing director of consultants, Hay Group UK observes:

The context for creating wealth is different now. Throughout this century we have built huge enterprises across the developed world. We are no longer searching for new markets or trade routes; we are no longer building new industrial or service enterprises; we are no longer rebuilding this part of Europe after war. Wealth creation over the last century has been fuelled by these activities. The task of the 1990s will be to tap into these enormous enterprises and realise their true value. The future will involve continuous improvement where success is not so much about goal attainment, described by concrete targets, as about demonstrating qualities and behaviours associated with high performance.[4]

As corporate success has become submerged and confused, so too has the personal success of managers. Often, managers are given strategic and personal objectives whose only clarity is the date they expire. 'My personal objectives for the year are pretty vague – the only tangible aspect is the deadline. In the end, it's how you're viewed rather than what you do,' one manager recently lamented to *The Times*.[5]

Constant change, commercial chaos, is now the order of the day. The environment in which strategists work is in a state of perpetual flux. Management by Objectives, if it exists at all, can only work on extremely short-term or straightforward projects. It is no longer the catch-all solution to strategic problems.

MOVING BEYOND THE MAGIC FORMULA FOR SUCCESS

McDonald's founder, Ray Kroc, aphoristically observed: 'Nothing recedes like success'. His observation is more true than ever.

For managers, the elusive and short-lasting nature of success is only part of the challenge of the 1990s. They have to possess a more wide-ranging view and knowledge than ever before. Being aware of the business environment is now an integral part of management. Managers cannot, for example, assume that there will always be customers for their products or services. They can no longer take markets for granted or their place within them.

If managers or leaders are out of touch with the broader context, their strategies are worthless. When Mikhail Gorbachev returned to Moscow in 1991 after the failed coup against him, he proclaimed his belief in the power of the Communist Party to achieve change. His response manifestly failed to understand the world he now operated in. The environment had changed – in a matter of days – and the strategies he wished to develop in the future were rendered groundless. Basing strategies on the static world of history, Gorbachev quickly became consigned to history.

There are no longer any water-tight formulae – if there ever were. The conventional wisdom was that a small airline couldn't make money unless it undercut the competition and as a result offered poor service. Yet Virgin has shown that people wanted to fly at reasonable rates with an organisation that doesn't appear to be a monolith.

Even so, managers remain addicted to the latest formulae for success. Formulae and the assumptions they are based on provide insulation from the cold winds of change in business. Entire businesses were built around the assumption that the market would continue to grow in the 1980s. In the absence of strong data to the contrary, managers assumed that the world would remain as it was.

Analysing the past mistakes of the UK company, Tarmac, its new chief executive Neville Simms, said:

> *The centre did not believe its job was to create the strategic path for the divisions, it believed it would grow because the divisions would grow. And it didn't believe its job was to allocate the financial cake; its job was to bake a financial cake that was big enough to meet the aspirations of the divisions.*[6]

Allied to this, there is a disturbing tendency for companies and those who manage them to stampede in the same direction. If markets are bullish, they too become like bulls, no matter what. As they stampede, the trouble is that they often don't know the destination and nor do their neighbours in the pack. This was demonstrated in the 1980s when companies sought to conquer the world through acquisitions.

The UK engineering group, Hawker Siddeley (now part of BTR), was a typical member of the stampeding herd. Between 1985 and 1990, Hawker made some 50 acquisitions with an average value of £6 million. The emphasis on small acquisitions and a perverse combination of niche markets left the company with around 100 profit centres. Its interests covered everything from sheep-shearing equipment to electric motors and railway signalling. Many other large organisations followed a similar route, ending up with impressive portfolios and declining profits as they sought to make sense of their latest acquisition in the Latvian textile industry.

At the opposite end, some companies did express a more restrained perspective. Reflecting on the growth of Allied Dunbar, the then chairman Sir Mark Weinberg, commented: 'We started off as a mature company. All our senior people had worked together in a large life insurance company before. We aimed to become the market leader in ability not size.'[7] Instead of joining the pack, Allied Dunbar settled down to nurturing what it had already identified as its key competitive weapon, its people.

The tendency to follow the herd can perhaps be put down to the ability of managers to create strategy in retrospect. Half-way down a particular avenue, the strategy suddenly emerges. 'For line managers the best strategy is the one they can implement; the one which makes them look good,' said one, rather cynical, manager. 'Articulating your real goal and strategy is a very rare activity. People want to get into it. There is a belief that you need the adrenalin of action to really clear things up.'

The judgemental errors of the 1980s expansionists are nothing new. Managers are attracted to consensus in the same way as most people. Despite the talk of entre-preneurism, most managers still prefer the safe option backed by large amounts of supportive analysis.

The most ready source of such analysis is history. This can preclude looking to the future. Newspaper typesetters in the UK were united in their opposition to the introduction of new technology. The fact that electronic methods were already used in other countries did not upset their vehement opposition. They preferred to think that circumstances were different and, anyway, the changes were geographically distant from their own environment. They selected their data from the past in a particular location and reached apparently logical conclusions.

Other industries – coal mining and fishing to name but two – have demonstrated that a strong culture can create a barrier to data so that statistics are based on assumptions that are fundamentally incorrect.

Optimistic assumptions are not solely the preserve of Western businesses. After unstinting economic growth, Japan has begun to pay the price in the 1990s for assuming that growth would continue come what may. Nissan president Yoshifumi Tsuji recently admitted: 'Car manufacturers have set their investment plans on the understanding that the economy would continue to grow, but this is no longer appropriate.'[8] Other Japanese manufacturers had worked on the same premise and were left with few products to stimulate demand while interest in their core products had collapsed.

Hindsight provides 20–20 vision, but there are countless examples of blurred and blinkered corporate views of the future regarding the best scenario as the most likely one.

Truth is sometimes inconvenient; but, commercially it is always essential. 'Everybody wants to talk about growth, but few people want to talk about declining businesses. Too many managers refuse to face the ugly reality that they are in a dying business,'[9] says Kathryn Rudie Harrigan, author of *Strategic Flexibility*. Conditioned and trained to analyse positive and historical data – rather than insubstantial trends – managers have sought out the good news, preferring the magic formula of growth for all and always to decision-making.

When asked why his company went bust, Sir Freddie Laker said: 'I was borrowing money from 30 leading banks. How could they all be wrong? I'm only a simple businessman.' Reassured by consensus, Laker ignored the grim reality.

Businesses' attitude to innovation provides another insight into the group mentality. Despite all that has been written about letting loose entrepreneurial instincts, managers have consistently derided and ignored innovations. The history of business is littered with people with bright ideas who spent their lives championing them only to meet inglorious silence or let some business magpie make off with the idea. One inventor commented that the reaction of competitors to a particularly bright idea of his followed the pattern of 'ignore, ridicule, attack, copy, steal'.

Today, if ideas, products or services don't fit into a preconceived formula or strategy, managers must look again. They are not in business to exclude potential, but to acknowledge, identify and build on it.

CREATING CERTAINTY FROM CHAOS

Analysis is no longer sufficient to create and implement strategy. The day of the analyst-chief executive is over. Now, senior managers need to be not only technically proficient (able to understand the potential and limitations of analysis), but also able to interpret information and take in the broader picture.

For managers, reformulating the way strategy works and the way it is organised, offers daunting challenges. They, after all, have been the guardians of all things strategic and have succeeded in championing strategy to the extent that it now amounts to a significant part of their work. As Howell Schroeder, director of Ashridge Management College's Strategic Management Programme, says:

> Strategy was once regarded as the preserve of the highest echelons of management – chief executives, directors and strategic planning managers. Companies tried to control the key decisions within an enclave. Now, as layers of hierarchy are shed, strategy is being driven down the organisation. The pace of change is fast. The trouble for many organisations is that chief executives are not necessarily very happy at abdicating responsibility for strategic decisions.

Chief executives are in an unsettling and paradoxical situation. They want to feel involved in the future direction of their organisation. They do not want to surrender all control to allow strategy to be a bottom-up process. But, it is apparent to them that a top-down process is risky in times of continuous change. Their job, therefore, is to provide some kind of balance between the two approaches and to recognise that, like the tightrope walker, you must continually shift your own weight in order to balance the entire structure. The balance must not be so precarious that unexpected forces or interruptions dislocate the mechanism.

The nature of the balancing act was observed by a colleague of high performer Ken Lawrie. 'I have no fixed job description,' he told us. 'I have to make sure our short-term targets don't compromise long-term goals. In practice, I deal with short-term issues and Ken takes the long-term ones.' Vague and uncertain though this seems, it is as clear a definition as is now possible.

A survey of the priorities of businesses by Korn Ferry[10] interestingly found that larger and smaller companies both shared the same two top priorities: cash flow and defining five-year strategy. The dichotomy between the two is striking – one of utmost practical immediacy, the other dealing with the strategies of the future.

It is this sort of gulf which managers are continually seeking to bridge, flitting desperately from strategic questions to worries about a customer's cheque arriving before the banks close.

Bridging the gap means that the fundamental role of managers is changing. From controllers, managers are now becoming enablers and facilitators. In an interview in the *Harvard Business Review*, Robert Haas of Levi Strauss commented:

> *If the people on the front line really are the keys to our success, then the manager's job is to help those people, the people that they serve. That goes against the traditional assumption that the manager is in control. In the past, a manager was expected to know everything that was going on and to be deeply involved in subordinate's activities.*[11]

Of course, in reality, it has always been something of a myth that managers are all-knowing and omnipotent. Their role is often deeply bedded in vagueness. The chief executive of a major company we talked to admitted that his desk was continually filled with reports, memos and corporate detritus which others simply passed on as they were unsure who should handle them. He saw his role as clarifying the grey areas. He decided who should handle each subject and passed the paper to them. He measured his general effectiveness by the number of times he had to intervene in problems and how often people responded to his comments with 'Yes, but . . . .' He wanted to cut out uncertainty as much as possible.

Civil servant John Michaels sums up his role in similar fashion. With a staff of tens of thousands and a budget of billions of pounds, he said: 'One of my key tasks is to bring some certainty to the major players.' Instead of being certain, managers now have to create certainty. Instead of laying down strategy, they have to synthesise many diverse strands of strategy. John Michaels regards his role as that of an integrator, someone who opens doors so everyone can become involved and articulate their ideas as strategy is formulated.

STRATEGY THAT WORKS

Brazil had one of the greatest football teams the world has ever seen entered in the 1970 World Cup. Watching them play, you could see total mastery of technique, teamwork and flexibility. Their game-plan – their strategy – evolved to fit the demands of the opposition while making the most of their skills. They found weaknesses in their opponents and adapted their style to capitalise on them. They changed formation to an extent that totally outwitted their opponents.

The free-flowing Brazilian approach has never since been emulated – although many have tried to do so. Instead, teams concentrate on creating a structure for themselves, an unbending approach based on knowing where their strengths and weaknesses lie. They may then tinker with this to fit the needs of a particular match, but it usually remains rigidly in place. If circumstances drastically change, they fail to respond.

In corporate terms the traditional approach to strategy has tended to separate the skills required to develop strategy in the first place (analytical) from those needed to achieve its objectives in reality (practical). This approach imagines the Brazilian team and then can't understand why it produces a team lacking in technique, coherence and inspiration.

The divide between analysis and practice is patently artificial – strategy does not stop and start, it is a continuous process of re-definition and implementation.

In an ideal world, the conventional approach follows a simple linear pattern:

Analysis   ⟹   Strategy   ⟹   Implementation

The deficiencies of this formula have been rigorously exposed by Kenichi Ohmae in *The Mind of the Strategist*:

> *Phenomena and events in the real world do not always fit a linear model. Hence the most reliable means of dissecting a situation into its constituent parts and reassembling them in the desired pattern is not a step-by-step methodology such as systems analysis. Rather, it is that ultimate non-linear thinking tool, the human brain.*[12]

Managers brought up on a diet of analysis have eventually had to accept that no data is foolproof. Some element of risk, imprecision or sheer guesswork is always evident. 'I like to believe that you can measure 80 per cent of a piece of string and just make a guess at the rest of it,' says Neville Simms, chief executive of Tarmac.[13] (After this comment, a correspondent observed that if Simms was clever enough to calculate 80 per cent of a piece of string he should have been able to quantify the remainder.)

The apparently simple chain of events from strategy to measurable success inevitably hits obstacles (see Figure 3.5).

For the high performers, data and analysis were regarded as a direct route to action rather than an obstacle or an end in

Figure 3.5 Obstacles to avoid on the strategy route

themselves. Often the managers saw their role as clearing the way for incontrovertible data to make its way across the organisation. IBM head Lou Gerstner has said: 'Once I have a feeling for the choices, I have no problems with the decisions.[14] There is something of this approach in the outlook of the high performers.

Taking over a struggling and disorganised group of companies, Tarmac's Neville Simms observed: 'There was such a strong feeling that something had to happen, that deciding what had to happen wasn't as difficult as you might imagine.'[15] The information was there for all to see; to a large extent, so too were the necessary decisions and the action.

Achieving this 'strong feeling' was seen as all-important by the high performers. Their belief was that accurate perception is more important than reams of data. Good perception brought answers by its very existence.

'My idea was that if you could provide it [a strategic plan] in a way that was completely transparent, the actions that were necessary would scream out from the data,' said multinational executive David Andrews.

Instead of corporately generated analysis, built around formulae, the high performers experienced a continuous process of personal analysis (see Figure 3.6). The personal analysis involved a huge amount of information and perceptions:

- *Current situation*: Through their ability to behave like a fish in water, the high performers were continually in touch with what was happening in the organisation.
- *Opinions*: They listened to opinions and made themselves available to colleagues and subordinates. This was more than a question of leaving their office door open – they

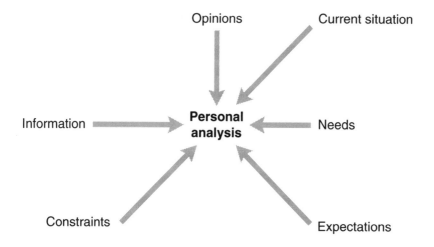

Figure 3.6 The continuous process of personal analysis

proactively canvassed opinions.

- *Information*: Fed a constant diet of information they had the ability to distill it down to its essence.
- *Expectations*: Their vision of the company was a constant companion, but one that changed with the problems and issues as they emerged. They were also keenly aware of what others expected from a particular project.
- *Needs*: In the short term, they had acute awareness of what the organisation, individuals and themselves required from a particular situation.
- *Constraints*: Part of their function was to encourage ideas, but ensure that they were tempered by commercial reality.

In practice this meant that they could act quickly and were not reliant on an endless stream of data to back up their perception. Catrina Carlberg worked with a small amount of information, but fitted it into her intuition and perception. She was not disabled by not knowing everything about a particular project. Her basic approach could be summarised as:

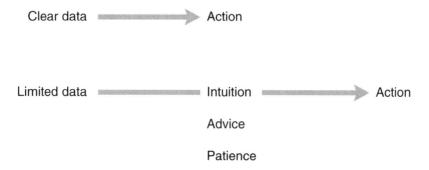

The more conventional manager would have stayed rooted to the spot, waiting for the clear data, before moving on to take action.

For the high performers it was not a simple matter of weighing up the facts – as directed. They were more comfortable talking about perceptions rather than decisions. This could be misinterpreted as a bias towards inaction. In reality, they were emphasising that individual decisions are merely the staging posts along the way towards clearly perceived goals.

The key simplicities were central to their ability to receive and send messages (see Figures 3.7 and 3.8).

For these managers strategy was practical and on-going. As Ken Lawrie observed:

You end up with a nicely prepared document which is a strategy, which is out-of-date from the moment it was written, because it's about uncertainty and being able to cope with uncertainty. The process of getting to that document, particularly with a very decentralised organisation without a big central staff, is much more about talking to people and getting them committed to the

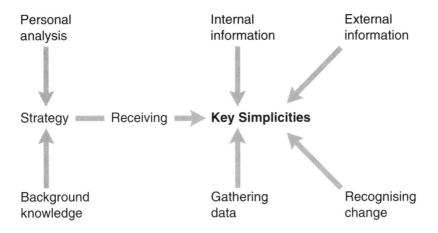

Figure 3.7   Receiving messages

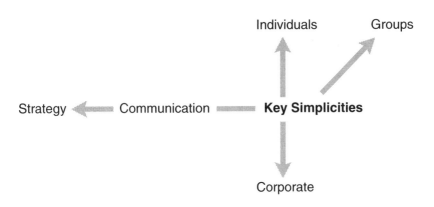

Figure 3.8 Sending messages

broad direction of the business and the broad issues of research allocation, rather than getting commitment to forecasts to the nearest penny. It is necessarily a disorganised process.

One of our companies has a central team that puts together a strategic model. They try out the strategic model on people in the field. But the last model was not owned by anyone. People started

*by saying we can't achieve that; you've imposed it upon us, we
don't want it. What I'm trying to do is produce something people
feel comfortable with and that they feel they have played a role in.
It might not deliver exactly what they want but they believe it is
achievable, it's sensible and it's been thought through and well
communicated. And the process of communication is untidy.*

As Ken Lawrie points out, the route from strategy to action is
quirky. Instead of being a clinical progression from A to B,
what emerges is an untidy journey full of distractions. It is,
however, a journey which can be made. Here is how two
managers in traditional manufacturing industries saw the
strategic light, but were not blinded and converted ideas into
practice.

Strategy that works: CV Carpets

Recently appointed as managing director, Malcolm Gibson,
decided that his company, CV Carpets (part of the Coats
Viyella Carpet Group), had a communication problem. The
solution, he believed, would be to take a group of senior
managers away for two days to examine how they went about
communicating. As he sat down and considered what they
should discuss, a more fundamental problem became clear to
him – 'We didn't have a strategy or a clear idea of where we
were going or what we needed to do. There was nothing to
communicate.'

The lack of any clear direction was partly explained by the
sheer complexity of CV's commercial situation. The carpet
industry is highly fragmented. There is no major branding
and, to compound the problem, the business is cyclical and

closely related to the health of the housing market. A carpet is a deferrable purchase and, when times are tough, more easily deferred.

Achieving change – making sure that strategy was communicated and implemented – involved Gibson taking a long hard look at his own skills as well as those in the company as a whole. He has an intimate operational knowledge of the carpet business and lengthy experience with CV. A PhD research scientist, he has worked in product development, quality control and purchasing, as well as sales and marketing. Becoming managing director in 1989, however, threw up areas where Gibson realised that he needed to know more if the business was to develop in a planned and sustained way. He recalls:

> *Though I understood the operational side, the industry and the business needed a much clearer strategic view of where we should go. We didn't have a long-term strategic vision. We were reacting to the environment rather than managing our own destiny.*

Instead of becoming more in-tune with a rapidly changing marketplace, managers had concentrated on settling into the new organisational structure, preferring to move plant around rather than tackling important strategic issues. The continuing existence of markets and customers was all but assumed. Gibson observes:

> *It is not unique to our business that it has a tendency to become very insular and introverted. Managers are much happier dealing with day-to-day issues rather than facing up to demanding questions about their long-term objectives, in terms of product, price, distribution and promotion.*

Though the will to change was increasingly evident, the skills to manage, control and sustain it were not in place. Gibson was keen to develop things further and broaden his own strategic knowledge so that he could lead the way. He argues that 'the background of recession was appropriate to the changes'. The market was going to become even tougher to survive in, and CV needed to be ready to meet the challenge.

Taking a three-week break from the business, Gibson went on a strategic management course. His aim was to provide himself with the tools to give CV the structure to develop a strategy for the business. Returning to work with his newly acquired skills, Gibson set about fleshing out the strategic plan and bringing other senior managers into the process.

> *We wanted it to be robust so that managers could look at strategy in the context of their own businesses and identify new directions. Our aim was to stand back and be able to identify objectively the major issues and opportunities affecting our business to create sustainable competitive advantage.*

A two-day strategy workshop involving 24 managers and representatives from the various parts of the business, developed the ideas further. Says Gibson:

> *We agreed that our strategy had to add value, reduce costs and the amount of capital employed, and that this required a cohesive culture. We then established teams to look at these key areas.*

It is, Gibson points out, 'not a quick fix. Strategy has to be part of a vision of where you want to go'. The process is continuous with long-term strategies continually being monitored and re-appraised.

> *It is cascading right through the business. Various cells, departments and units are now coming up with their own embellishments to the basic ideas. In time, it will become self-generating.*

Involving all the company's employees in strategy involves a wide variety of initiatives. When asked for ideas to improve performance, CV employees at Donaghadee came up with 2,097 – six per employee. Multi-disciplined teams are now used continually. Customers are now closer to the company – they meet people other than sales staff – and the service they receive is improved. The Skelmersdale plant aims to process and dispatch orders in less than 24 hours. Customer complaints are substantially down.

'The benefits of clear-sighted strategic planning are already having an affect on the bottom-line of the business,' says Malcolm Gibson. Production at Donaghadee, for example, has reached 110,000 square metres of carpet a day. In the not so distant past, this took a week.

Suppliers have been brought into the strategy process.

Managing the supply chain is vital in improving effectiveness. So we set about treating suppliers as strategic allies. It was a concept which initially startled them. They weren't used to being recognised as an integral part of our business. In practice it means we don't have to commit ourselves to buying yarn too early and that our sales people have more flexibility. For the suppliers, it means they manage their businesses more as they want and when. The lead-time for raw materials is now down to two weeks.

The strategic process helps you to become much more aware of the wider commercial environment. That, in itself, helps people to become more critical of their own and the company's performance. Most strategic plans are images without substance. We have had to come up with an image of the future of our company and business. Now, we also have the substance to back it up.

Strategy that works: Charnos

Charnos is the archetypal manufacturing company in an

archetypal manufacturing town, Ilkeston in Derbyshire. The town's biggest employer, Charnos has been producing lingerie, hosiery and knitwear for over fifty years. As many other companies and towns have discovered, traditional manufacturing brings with it its own hefty baggage of entrenched working practices and blinkered thinking. Why change when you have been working the same way for decades? While some managers have simply shrugged their shoulders and refused to countenance change, those at Charnos have been working hard at transforming tradition.

Graeme Morris, deputy managing director of Charnos' knitwear division, has championed a radical change of attitude. His bugbear is the not uncommon problem of 'functional silos': units, groups and departments built on their own isolation from the rest of the company.

The realisation that this was a major and long-standing problem came when Morris looked at other organisations he dealt with.

They were actually making our job harder and, often, creating confusion. I saw that their problems were rooted in the fact that different parts of their organisations often failed to communicate with each other as well as those they dealt with externally. I then began to look at the way Charnos was organised. I knew divisions existed and people worked in their own compartments. But, as I looked closer, I saw that we had our own functional silos. We had quality and technical, knitting, making-up, production control, purchasing and design and development. There weren't any walls of stone, but there was a failure to communicate or share ideas. People were often unwilling to take responsibility for their actions. They would simply blame another department. With this outlook, you end up blaming a sheep in Australia.

Morris learnt more about strategic planning and set about

changing things – making it clear that he, too, bore some
responsibility.

*I have worked my way up through the company and I'm sure that
I have actually used and created silos to take a step forward. It is
part of what was once a permissible technique of management:
divide and conquer.*

Morris regards this newly acquired objectivity as a central
managerial skill.

*Though I had grown up in the business, my management style
needed refinement. There is a great deal of benefit in realising that
all businesses face similar types of problems. If you have the
knowledge of strategic management it doesn't change the way you
manage, but allows you to explain some decisions and sub-
consciously the knowledge is always at work.*

The first stage in breaking down the invisible but historical
barriers was to call 60 of the 700 workforce together and
explain the concept.

*The key thing was that people recognised the silos. Often they had
created them themselves or found that they were continually
banging their heads against them.*

What Morris was doing, through his candour about his own
responsibility, was bringing the unspoken into the open. 'If
you admit it, you are encouraging people to change.'

Demolishing the silos, he explains, was simple enough.
'Every time I saw evidence of a silo, I would draw people's
attention to it.' The message has been well received. Walking
down the corridor, Morris looks into each office and asks the
managers what they do with functional silos. The response,
which would not amuse pacifists, pleases Morris.

*What I hoped to achieve was cross-fertilisation of ideas and
communication of information and advice. This is happening,*

though there are always going to be people who are so steeped in the old culture that they find it hard to adapt to change.

The business reasons for breaking the barriers are as straightforward as Morris' approach.

Our raw material is highly flexible. While in car making, for example, there is a specified and rigid way of doing things, we have a whole range of variables. Different coloured yarn might react in a different way, so we have to be able to adjust and refine our way of working to get the best result.

With greater flexibility, backed with closer relationships with customers and the disappearance of functional silos, Charnos is actually meeting its targets.

We have been able to achieve what we set out to do because we take time to look at how we are performing and where we are going and monitor achievements continually. In the past, targets were plucked from the air.

With an influx of new managers, Morris believes the company's thinking has been changed permanently. 'Sharing and communicating will become second nature. Functional silos will soon become things of the past.'

Strategy that works: before and after

High-performance strategy	Conventional strategy
Accepts uncertainty as a fact of business life.	Creates certainties no matter what the external situation.
Continually looks outside the organisation to learn lessons and improve effectiveness.	Looks inwards and dismisses the experiences of others.

High-performance strategy	Conventional strategy
Learns from past mistakes and achievements.	Regards the past as dead and buried.
Uses unconventional images to communicate strategic initiatives.	Looks upon imagery as needless frippery.
Produces short, highly informative strategy documents.	Labours long and hard to produce epic bound volumes.
Regards strategy as a business tool.	Elevates strategy to godlike status as *the* business tool.
Does not allow pre-conceived ideas to interfere with honest interpretation.	Believes that events are always driven by strategy.
Distrusts immediate concensus.	Encourages immediate concensus.
Is prepared to put faith in 'strong feelings' and takes risks.	Dismisses emotional data.
Assumes nothing.	Assumes nothing has changed.
Breaks down barriers.	Erects and sanctions barriers.
Is generated by generalists.	Is the sole preserve of specialists.
Involves everyone.	Involves as few people as possible.
Challenges.	Stagnates.

References

1 KPMG Management Consulting, *Change Management*, KPMG, 1993.
2 Reported in Stuart Crainer, *Zeebrugge: Learning from disaster*, HFA, 1993.
3 Igor Ansoff, quoted in David Clutterbuck and Stuart Crainer, *Makers of Management*, Macmillan, 1990.
4 A Mitrani, M Dalziel and D Fitt, *Competency Based Human Resource Management*, Kogan Page, 1992.
5 Jean-Louis Barsoux, 'Living up to expectations', *The Times*, 20 May 1993.

6 Heather Connon, 'A solid brick in the wall', *Independent on Sunday*, 25 April 1993.

7 Mark Weinberg, 'How marketing sharpened Allied Dunbar's edge', *Marketing Business*, June 1989.

8 Michiyo Nakamoto, 'Beating an orderly retreat', *Financial Times*, 30 July 1993.

9 Interview with Kathryn Rudie Harrigan, 1989.

10 Korn Ferry UK, *Board of Directors Survey*, 1992.

11 Robert Haas, 'Values make the company', *Harvard Business Review*, September/October 1990.

12 Kenichi Ohmae, *The Mind of the Strategist*, McGraw Hill, 1982.

13 Neville Simms, 'A solid brick in the wall', *Independent on Sunday*, 25 April 1993.

14 Lou Gerstner, 'The inconoclast at IBM', *Independent on Sunday*, 1 August 1993.

15 Neville Simms, 'A solid brick in the wall', *Independent on Sunday*, 25 April 1993.

4

HIGH PERFORMANCE
INTEGRATED

**High performance demands a pot-pourri of
skills, sensitivities and awareness. It pulls
together and integrates a wide range of
management skills rather than treating them
as mutually exclusive.**

Learning to learn
Learning is often regarded as something which senior managers do not do. Now, more than ever, they must learn to learn.

Making sense of the past
How can managers learn from the past when all they remember is a jumble of unrelated facts and experiences as intertwined as a plate of spaghetti?

Recognising synchronicity
With no winners and uniqueness disappearing, the search for synchronicity begins.

How high performers make intuition work
How high performers recognise and capitalise on their own intuition.

The leader as resource
More than a boss or a colleague, the manager now needs to be a corporate resource and problem-solver.

Using obsession
How high performers manage obsessiveness to achieve results.

Getting the message across
Cutting through the tautology of management-speak, high performers communicate directly and effectively.

Questioning and self-awareness
Though confident and self-aware, high performers always want to know more.

Measuring success
To the high performers success is not cut and dried or a purely financial measurement. It is more to do with progress than pounds.

Initial analysis of the high performers showed that the more obvious elements of their managerial style were:

- awareness of their fallibility;
- clarity and action;
- commitment and energy;
- key simplicities;
- contributing as leader;
- complete fluency with their environment – behaving as a fish in water.

In addition to these basic skills and characteristics many more elements are at work. As the high performers emphasise, strategy is an untidy process. While the above are the foundations of high performance, without which it is unlikely any manager will achieve it, high performance demands other critical elements. The end-result is not a rag-bag of skills, but various groupings and combinations of skills and approaches which are integrated and constantly utilised and supplemented.

LEARNING TO LEARN

In previous centuries the dominant thinkers and influences on the way people lived were kings, clerics, diplomats, lawyers, generals and scientists. Our perception of history is dotted with the key figures we first encountered in school textbooks. No matter where you were educated or what books you studied, it is unlikely that any managers featured in the Pantheon of historical greats.

Even so, it is worth adding that management is an ancient discipline. Peter Drucker sagely observes:

> *The CEO of Pyramids Inc who built the Cheops pyramid 6,000 years ago surely knew more about management than any CEO of today. And so did whoever conceived, planned and managed the cave of Ajanta in India (which carried out a master plan for 600 years without making a single mistake) or, even much earlier, whoever designed and managed the prehistoric cave paintings in Spain and in the Dordogne Valley of France.*[1]

While people have been practising management from time immemorial, it is only in this century that management has become recognised as a discipline. Alongside this has been the recognition that management, like the historical professions, needs to make use of study and learning if it is to become more effective and continue its development. Management, however, is not a stationary instinctive discipline, but technological, innovative, flexible, specialist and generalist.

The initial response to encourage managers to learn more was to construct syllabuses in the style of those used in other professions. Now, with the parameters of management expanding and the pressure on managers intensifying, it is clear that nothing as simple as a syllabus will suffice to guide managers in their study and learning. They must develop new ways of learning – they must learn to learn – in order to cope with a business environment in a state of flux.

The highly structured and compartmentalised approach is now criticised increasingly. 'Business schools don't teach you anything about people,' laments Alan Bowkett, chief executive of Berisford International, who also has an MBA.

'At Boulton & Paul [a company he helped turn round] I had to change attitudes, getting people to participate and breaking down the us-and-them attitude. If you are suddenly making someone work till eight at night, they and their spouses have to know why.'[2]

A 1993 report, *On Course for Success*, by the Economist Intelligence Unit[3] displays the failure of management education. Among the criticisms levelled at management education providers are:

- Teaching faculties are overbearing and patronising in their approach. Companies question why they should learn from professors who themselves only learn from books.
- Faculties assume that they are there to teach and put little effort into finding out how the organisation goes about things, even when they are working with tailored clients.
- Too many providers are trying to be all things to all people and are in danger of losing their way.
- While many providers and their customers believe that forging partnerships is the way ahead, providers have to do more than give off-the-shelf packages 'facelifts' to make them appear more customised.

With carefully constructed syllabuses, business schools have preferred to train managers in techniques and methods. As a result, managers have come to believe that the more techniques they acquire, the better and more effective managers they become.

This perception continues among some commentators . In his recent book *Managing to Survive*, Sir John Harvey-Jones writes:

Most ideas on management have been around for a very long time, and the skill of the manager consists in knowing them all and, rather as he might choose the appropriate golf club for a particular situation, choosing the particular ideas which are most appropriate for the position and time in which he finds himself.[4]

The trouble is that, unlike golf, management cannot be handled one hole at a time; it is a team game involving various numbers and groupings of players. Also, the bag of skills required by the modern manager would need to be extremely large, so large that he would probably collapse at the first tee.

Perhaps nearer the truth for the manager of the 1990s is Frederick Herzberg's observation: 'We need Renaissance men as managers – broadly educated men who can see the inter-relationships of sociology, psychology, technical aspects.'[5] (Both Harvey-Jones and Herzberg appear to assume that management remains a male domain!)

Business schools would be quick to rebut many of the accusations of being out of touch and overly structured. Undoubtedly they are changing both in approach and outlook as they realise that the effective manager is not a narrow creature consisting of a bundle of hastily learned techniques. Business schools now need to educate as much as train. They have to stop teaching management and begin to teach managers.

Letting go of the sides

The human body floats in water, whether it is dead or alive. Yet, we continue to teach people to swim when, in reality, we're merely teaching them how to let go of the sides of the pool. Attitudes to learning are an integral part of achieving high performance.

In a *Harvard Business Review* article, Chris Argyris observed:

> *Any company that aspires to succeed in the tougher business environment of the 1990s must first resolve a basic dilemma: success in the marketplace increasingly depends on learning, yet most people don't know how to learn. What's more, those members of the organisation that many assume to be the best at learning are, in fact, not very good at it.*[6]

For a great many – perhaps the majority – of senior managers, learning isn't regarded as part of what they do. There are too many managers with ten years' experience who have simply had one year's experience ten times.

'Success ought to be evidence of learning,' said one manager, adding, 'the trouble is it usually isn't. For managers learning is often a defensive reaction to failure. You will hear managers saying something is an opportunity to learn when someone they don't like has been made their boss and they can't afford to leave.' Learning is done under sufferance or as a penalty for perceived failure.

Given their exhortations for governments to support training at all levels and protestations that their companies invest heavily in training, it is a little ironic that senior managers are routinely passed by on the annual training round.

'There was always the assumption that because you had reached an elevated level you could do certain things. You had, in effect, finished learning,' says Patricia Marshall, director of management consultants Hay/McBer. 'Now, people are more open about being unable to carry out particular tasks and learning is regarded as lifelong.'[7]

Their career progression often bears this out. Many managers become proficient in one particular area early in their careers. This brings them to someone's attention and they are put in a more elevated position to provide more of the same. If the results and their performance are predictable and reliable, then they will progress still further. This pattern emphasises implementation rather than actually learning from the tasks. Talking to senior managers it is notable that those who appear to learn from implementation began to do so early in their career.

As an adjunct to this, there is a tendency among managers to be dismissive of the past. Instead of learning from it, they often appear to regard it as historical and insignificant. They like to be seen as people for the moment and the future rather than preservers of the past.

Unfortunately, in practice this means that mistakes are repeated and botched jobs botched again in the vain hope of a solution emerging. 'You can't say, "I just can't do it," and hope everything will be fine,' said Mike Sutcliffe. 'You've got to say, "I think this is right. Now, I've got to find out what actually matters within the solution". You go from a very wide to a very tight focus.'

In fact, managers appear poorly equipped to recognise when they are learning. After six months of intensive coaching it is quite common for managers to learn a great deal and then claim that the knowledge was already there in the first place! Appraisals and assessments are generally notable for their lack of impact.

'Traditionally, assessment has been something *done* to individuals,' say Kevin Barham and Elizabeth Braiden of Ashridge Management College. 'If individuals are to change and develop, however, it is important that individuals take ownership of the assessment and are able to use and build on active feedback. A capacity for self-review and for realistic self-assessment is a fundamental part of the ability to put aside assumptions and to learn.'[8]

A survey of over 100 top UK companies by management consultants Coopers & Lybrand noted:

> *Our view is that appraisal systems in many companies are not resulting in action to tackle the crucial issue of the development of people and their skills, and are in danger of becoming no more than an annual ritual. That is in spite of the increasing recognition of the growing demands on managers.*[9]

The research found that only 40 per cent of companies had definite arrangements in place to ensure that all of their managers had the skills needed to operate effectively – even though almost all the companies operated some form of performance management or appraisal system.

Part of the problem is that learning is impossible to quantify. Managers are unhappy with this elusiveness. They are used to evaluating input and output. This is exacerbated the further you move up the corporate hierarchy. Lower down it is relatively straightforward to take a sample of someone's work, train them and then test again. At a senior level there is often nothing you can count or measure at the end of a day. Discomforted by this, managers take solace in measuring the number of hours they work rather than their effectiveness. When two managers meet they are likely to greet each other with the information, 'I'm very busy', taking activity to imply effectiveness.

How can managers learn?

1. Finding the right situation

On a management course one person stood out. She was a

consultant at a leading hospital. As well as a plethora of qualifications, involvement in many organisations and professional bodies, she was a highly talented pianist. Asked to choose an assignment, she selected writing an action plan for re-organising a particular work unit. The result was impressive – the only typed piece of work, coherent and accurate.

When questioned, she admitted that the action plan was an easy thing for her to do – she had prepared many similar plans in her professional capacity. Despite her achievements and skills, she was highly defensive about putting herself in new situations, areas where she knew she did not speak with authority or have lengthy experience to fall back on. The action plan had, in fact, taught her nothing.

To move forward and develop as individuals and managers, managers must put themselves in situations where they can learn. In fact, they probably already do so – only they do not recognise it.

Explaining his learning processes, Ken Lawrie said: 'I think about things that have gone badly. I think about why. I talk to people I trust about these things. I want to have a fairly meticulous plan and have things set out. It may sound vague but for me it is meticulous. You've got to spend time with bright, committed people, explaining why some ideas are carried through and what they should be thinking. It's like coaching.'

But who coaches the senior manager? Ken admitted: 'In general, no-one, but in specifics, anyone – my managers, for example, critique my presentations and help me to get it right.' Though the manager has clear ideas about what he wishes to achieve, he is willing to learn from anyone along the way so that his ideas can be modified and improved.

2. Using mistakes

For fifteen years American academic Chris Argyris examined the behaviour of management consultants. Highly trained, well paid and apparently successful, Argyris discovered that the majority of the consultants were poorly equipped to learn from experience and, in particular, errors. 'Because many professionals are almost always successful at what they do, they rarely experience failure. And because they have rarely failed, they have never learned how to learn from failure,'[10] he concluded. Instead of being able to identify and admit mistakes and shortcomings, Argyris found that the consultants became highly defensive, passing the blame to clients and senior managers.

Managers fed on a diet of corporate politics are highly adept at covering their footsteps. More often than not, mistakes are covered up and concealed rather than learned from.

American psychologist David McClelland divides people into two broad categories. The first are those motivated by a need for positive achievement. They tend to look on their errors as an opportunity to do better next time. The others, motivated by fear of failure, are typically preoccupied by the need to avoid making mistakes.

In fact, the only thing managers have to fear is fear itself. Psychologist Michael Frese of Giessen University in Germany has carried out research into mistake-making. He concludes that pressure leads to mistakes; more pressure, more mistakes. In training, he suggests, people should be set tasks so complicated that they are bound to make mistakes. The result, says Frese, is that people learn more complex skills faster and, though errors are made, their effects are less damaging.

Being able to cope with and build on painful experiences is a crucial aspect of learning and of high performance. Reflecting on an early failure, Dr Christina Townsend, chief executive of the National Health Service Training Directorate, reflected: 'Living with the discomfort of not doing well is always hard to bear – but if I hadn't gone through it, I probably would have played it safe for most of my career and would not have ended up in the job I now hold.'[11]

Learning from adversity and error is something which corporations have long-acknowledged. Sending youthful managers to distant outposts of corporate empires is standard practice. It is similar to throwing a non-swimmer into the deep end and then walking away. Learning is assumed. So too is the manager's ability to learn from the experience and mistakes he or she makes.

3. Looking beyond the office

Managers also need to learn from external experiences. Increasingly, managers are looking beyong the narrow confines of their companies and colleagues to learn the lessons which will improve their performance. We see, for example, that public sector organisations now encompass private sector skills in their management. Indeed, many public sector managers are now studying for MBAs and other conventional management qualifications.

Pauline Tagg is associate business development manager at Doncaster Royal Infirmary. A former nurse, she is now studying for an MBA. The logic, she explains, is simple. 'Managers have the same problems. Those in the private sector don't seem to be any better at solving them than we are. We too have to deal with scarcity of resources, rationalisation, communications and effective business planning.'[12]

Learning from other areas of commerce and society is growing in importance. David Grayson of Business in the Community says:

> *The revolution at all levels in society requires new partnerships so that different sectors can learn from each other. There must be a willingness to experiment with new forms of delivery of public services. The key words and ideas of this new structure must be flexibility, adaptability and empowerment. We must be receptive to learning, achieving more with less resources, through the mobilisation of partnerships in all sectors of society.*[13]

4. Accepting chance

'I want lucky people. The luckier my managers are, the better I like it,' John Moores, founder of the Littlewoods empire, is reputed to have said.[14]

If managers are prepared to learn from elsewhere, they need also to accept that learning is often far from systematic. It is, instead, sometimes a matter of chance. Again, the element of chance rests uneasily with the case study method of learning.

One good example of the flawed case study approach has been exposed by Richard Pascale, author of *Managing on the Edge*. Honda's move into the American motorbike market was heralded by a consultant's report to a competitor as a triumph of rational management. But, reported by one of Honda's people who was actually there, it was based on chance and a lack of knowledge about the market. However, this was backed by a preparedness to learn, experiment and turn a strategy upside down to reflect the real situation. What seems, on paper at least, to be a model of strategy when told later was at the time a confused tale of initial misjudgement and seizing an opportunity even though it went against what bosses and head office wanted.[15]

How do managers learn?

Part of the problem is that managers are not normally aware of how they learn. They receive information, but regard it as a disposable short-term tool to achieve a particular task rather than as an addition to their long-term weaponry. The process of learning can be neatly summarised: we take data, manipulate it and call it information; we take information, manipulate it and call it learning; we take learning, manipulate it and call it wisdom (see Figure 4.1).

Managers have tended to concentrate on the first stages of the process. They are good at delegating to others to collect data and facts. Many are excellent at distilling vast amounts of data into information. They are, however, less comfortable with the rest of the process. With the information at their fingertips they are keen to make it work – they are usually unwilling to accept that they have learned something and that that might be the end of that particular process. Equally, starved of hard facts and masses of data, they cannot achieve synthesis. They are uncomfortable if they have to take weak signals from the environment and pull them together. They demand certainty which learning, wisdom and judgement often fail to provide.

Fast track to learning

For many senior managers learning to learn requires that they return to basics. It can be done – first principles can be

Data

Facts

Information

Learning

Wisdom

Judgement

Figure 4.1

re-learned, re-evaluated and re-drawn. It is not a matter of unlearning but of unlocking your skills and knowledge.

As we learn a new skill we pass from unconscious incompetence (not knowing we can't do it) to conscious incompetence (knowing what we can't do). As learning progresses we move to conscious competence (we are aware that we are doing it – like someone learning to drive) and, finally, to unconscious competence (we do it without thinking) (see Figure 4.2).

Nick Faldo was among the world's best golfers in the

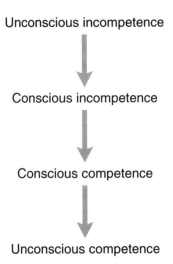

Figure 4.2 Learning a skill

mid-1980s. Despite his success, he was unhappy – he believed he could be the best. He carried on playing in tournaments but, every other minute available he was found with his coach completely re-building the way he played golf. Faldo went back to the basics; re-learned the game from first principles and emerged as the leading player in the world.

Talking of what it takes to get to the top Faldo has said: 'It requires more than having a good technique. It's about character as well. I don't know that you can put your finger on exactly what it takes to climb up to that level. And I don't know that you can easily see it from the outside.' But, commenting on another golfer who had failed to fulfil early promise, Faldo observed: 'He is practising to maintain his game rather than practising to improve it.'[16] Dedication to constant improvement is the key – stasis leads to stagnation.

The link with management is a tenuous one for most senior managers. They simply don't have the time to analyse every aspect of their managerial technique. Many have difficulty in accepting that their technique and style could be flawed in any serious way – it is successful, why change?

Jerry Cope, personnel director of the UK's Royal Mail, managed a massive assessment programme as part of his organisation's restructuring. He also went through the process of individual assessment.

Most managers have a keen idea of the negative side of the people who work for them. They know what people can't do. Often, however, they overlook the things people are good at. Sometimes they are completely unaware of people's skills. Individual assessment enabled us to look at ourselves, and our staff, to highlight the positive side and to develop areas where we were lacking. The aim was to identify the skills that existed in the organisation so that we knew which needed to be developed if we were to succeed in bringing about fundamental change.

So far, 12,000 people have been through the process.

Inevitably, such close analysis of how you work and think about your work is uncomfortable. But, if you are aware of the possible benefits and are honest, you can learn.[17]

Research in fifty of the world's leading companies by Philip Sadler and Keith Milmer highlighted ten important rules for the management of talent:

1. Provide a clear sense of direction and purpose for employees, developing and implementing a strong sense of mission.
2. Develop an appropriately flexible organisational framework, balancing control and creativity, and integrating different procedural and value systems.
3. Understand the company culture and nurture the talented people within it through the authority of

expertise, encouraging innovation and risk-taking, providing freedom, autonomy, space and flexibility, openness and trust, and a dedication to excellence.

4. Clearly identify future requirements for talent, both quantitatively and qualitatively.
5. Create a talent pool by developing recruitment and selection strategies.
6. Identify high potential.
7. Build ties of loyalty and commitment; these are often more important than financial incentives.
8. Set clear objectives and ensure that they are met, providing support at all levels.
9. Motivate and develop talented people.
10. Continuously evaluate the impact of human resource strategies in terms of cost-benefit analysis and employee attitudes and satisfaction.[18]

For organisations this checklist represents a series of formidable challenges for the future. For individual managers, development possibilities are now likely to play a far greater role in career decisions. It is, however, not simply a matter of sitting back and waiting to be developed; it, too, can be a highly unsettling experience.

Euan Cameron was a divisional director of UK rail company Network South East. A senior manager in a large organisation, he was at the forefront of a major restructuring.

> *The change to a divisional organisation involved completely disbanding and rebuilding the way we organised ourselves. Central to this process was the development of teams which could deliver what customers wanted. Instead of concentrating on input, we wanted to concentrate on output and ensure that it was channelled in the right direction.*

At a three-day team-building exercise, Euan's pre-conceptions about his role in the new team were rudely awakened.

> *What came out was that the rest of the team didn't like my management style. They thought I was autocratic, subject to mood swings and poor at delegating. It was hard to take. Effectively it was a rejection.*

Some may have shrugged their shoulders and carried on as before. The criticism was not accompanied by easy solutions. Euan, however, realised that he had to change if he was to play a leading role in the new rigorous process of self-appraisal and feedback. His managerial style was laid bare for all to see and comment on.

The appraisal process was nothing new to Euan. This time, however, it was taken a stage further.

> *In the past, appraisals confirmed what I already knew and were then filed away. I had the information, but did not seek a translation. This time I was coached to take the next step, presenting my findings back to the team as I progressed. I quickly began to move away from telling people what to do. Instead, I began to appreciate how different people worked and thought.*

The failure – or impotence – of appraisals is a common experience. 'The contribution of the management team as a whole is difficult to identify, never mind the input of any given individual,' says Jean-Louis Barsoux of Templeton College. 'Performance appraisals were contrived to make the process more objective, but in reality, they often serve to legitimise subjective judgements.'[19] Civil servant John Michaels, for example, had major problems in tackling an appraisal system designed by a central personnel department which his managers felt had little practical use and had been foisted upon them.

With an effective appraisal system and carefully monitored feedback, the emphasis of Euan Cameron's work was drastically altered. He spent more time on one-to-one meetings and was much less confrontational. He admits,

> *There was a degree of cynicism. But the response has become much more positive. I am now able to learn from things that go wrong rather than shouting louder the next time to make sure I get it right. I think I am playing to my strengths and am better able to take in the broader picture – it is no longer all black and white.*

Having witnessed Euan Cameron's willingness to re-learn his management style, the next stage was for functional managers to go through the same process so that it could cascade through the organisation.

> *There was a lot of hesitation before many took the plunge. It is one thing filling in forms, quite another to go through counselling and to present your findings to the rest of the team.*

For some, he admits, the message is unpalatable.

> *People with inadequacies are exposed. The manipulative are shown to be just that. But you can't afford to have people playing games. If the team is to succeed the dynamics of how it works must be understood by everyone, so it is clear how we all fit in and what we have to contribute.*

As Euan Cameron's experience testifies, learning to learn requires a great deal of commitment and honesty. He had to come to terms with his own inadequacies as a manager and completely re-build his approach. It is, however, not totally foolproof. Nick Faldo's form is subject to fluctuation as much as anyone's. The difference is that he has a level of understanding about what makes him perform well which enables him to identify and correct faults as they develop. By regarding learning as an integral part of what they do and utilising every opportunity to do so, managers might be able to follow Faldo's example.

How high performers learn to learn

- *Learning from past experience.* The high performers regard the past as a rich source of achievements to be emulated; mistakes to be learned from; and people who's own attitudes and approach can be learned from.
- *Acknowledging mobility.* Management and learning are never stationary. Today's accomplishments are tomorrow's failings; high performers manage to improve as managers, rather than managing to stay the same.
- *Integrating skills.* Learning is not solely a matter of adding more and more skills to your personal armoury. It is a question of what you do with them and how they work together.
- *Treating learning positively as an opportunity and necessity for all*, rather than as a last recourse in times of trouble.
- *Acknowledging learning as a key part of the managerial function*, not an optional extra.
- *Creating an environment in which individual learning is encouraged and cultivated.*
- *Learning from everyone and everything.*
- *Using assessment and appraisal systems* which are sensitive to the needs of the organisation and individuals, and which are active and continuous.

MAKING SENSE OF THE PAST

In an interview with Catrina Carlberg we asked her to try to remember what she had done three months earlier when we had last met. At that time she had had an exceptionally clear idea what she needed to do and what were the major milestones in the forthcoming weeks. But, asked to recall what had happened, she was blank. The date meant nothing – it was a chronological staging-post along the way to her business goals, but she could not fill in any more details. The past, apart from the scantiest of outlines, had disappeared from view.

Other managers appeared to have the same problem. When they were asked about their activities over the preceding weeks and months they too were often unable to remember. They would say, 'Well a lot has happened since we last spoke. I can't quite remember what it was, or in what order it happened. But, things have really moved on in those few weeks.' This does not sound particularly surprising, except that three weeks earlier the managers had been able to say what the four or five major items on their agenda were. Not only that – they could put them in order of importance and give dates for important meetings and decisions. Only a few weeks later and having lived through the events, they couldn't say what had happened without desperately searching through their diaries.

We were puzzled by this because, when prompted by their diary, the managers could remember a great deal of what had happened. But their memories were a mixture of data and the emotions attached to the data. As they looked at the recent past, they recalled emotions and feelings more strongly than concrete events, meetings or decisions (see Figure 4.3).

While the past was laden with emotions rather than events, the managers viewed the future in a completely different light. It was mapped out strictly in terms of dates and events (see Figure 4.4). Even so, research suggests that most people learn more from experience rather than from any structured training or teaching. This throws up the question of how managers can learn when the past appears to be a jumble of facts and emotional data with no structure?

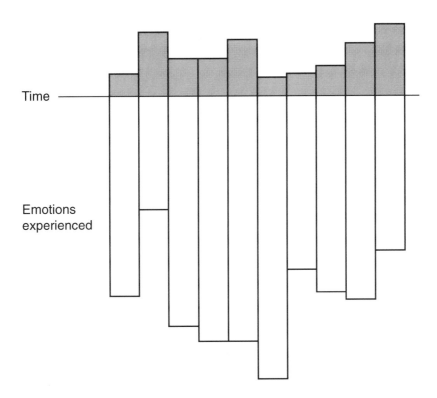

Figure 4.3 How managers saw the past

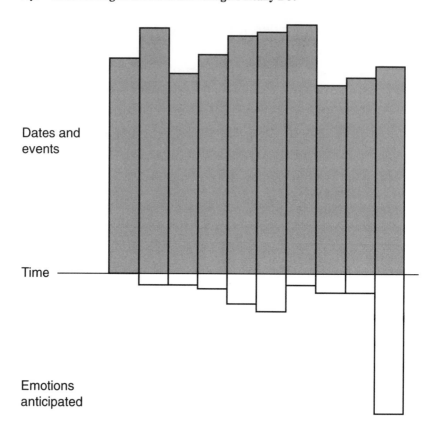

Figure 4.4 How managers saw the future

In turn, this again exposes the fallibility of the traditional case study method of management education. Case studies make management appear tidy and logical. Yet, in reality the thought processes are complex and jumbled. Finding a way through is as practical as unravelling a plate of spaghetti.

All the research on how managers actually spend their time suggests that amnesia is to some extent inevitable – rarely do they have the space or time to think.

The statistics in Table 4.1 show little difference in the way American and Japanese managers spend their time. There is,

Table 4.1 **How managers spend their time**[20]

	% US managers	% Japanese managers
Desk work	22	24
Telephone	6	1
Scheduled meetings	59	59
Tours	3	10
Others	10	6
Duration of activities		
Less than 9 minutes	49	4
Between 6 and 60 minutes	41	12
Longer than one hour	10	44

however, a great deal of difference in the duration of their activities. American managers spend a much larger part of their time dealing with things in short concentrated bursts. As any athlete will tell you it is short bursts which exhaust you the most.

The tendency to spend short periods of time on any one subject makes it even more unlikely that managers can gain a profitable perspective on the past. For managers the challenge is to make sense of the spaghetti, to learn from the confusion of history.

Among the high performers, the managers were adept at making the time to identify what they had learned. Although the immediate past was confused, they appeared able to integrate important lessons into their current thinking.

Their intuitive approach was summed up by Catrina Carlberg: 'The past is your database, like a picture book. You match the patterns you see before you to your mental picture book. You may not have thought about something before, but somehow you find that you knew it already.'

Instead of being dormant, the past is pillaged for its lessons, examples and inspiration.

Catrina also attempts to organise her time so that she can concentrate on key issues. The first two hours of every morning, she spends dealing with what she had identified as important topics demanding time and attention.

The experience of the high performers suggests that to make sense of the spaghetti managers need to:

- continually monitor and re-appraise progress;
- maintain clear sets of goals and targets, evaluating achievements as they occur;
- take time to learn from the lessons of the past, otherwise they will soon be lost;
- accept experience as a rich source of understanding and knowledge rather than as history;
- organise time effectively to spend concentrated periods on crucial issues rather than moving from subject to subject bringing your full concentration to bear only briefly.

RECOGNISING SYNCHRONICITY

Management writer Michael Porter argues that there are three basic ways an organisation can compete in any given market. It can be the lowest-cost producer; the differentiated producer charging more for the added value they bring to a particular product or service; or the occupier of a specialist niche.

Neatly compartmentalised though this sounds, the route to competitive advantage, in reality, is fraught with difficulty.

'I spent five years studying what sort of company I could create that required no capital, gave no credit, satisfied a demand and had no competition.'[21] Derek Wadlow is now managing director of Motivity. His quest for competitive uniqueness led him to create a company tackling everything from assembling sacks of sand for a board game to packing bags of goodies for athletes. Wadlow discovered that uniqueness lay in tedium. A company with a turnover of £750,000 was created out of ennui.

Many thousands of people are now involved in research and development aimed at helping their organisations to discover something unique. They can then steal a march on their competitors and capitalise on the years of careful preparatory work.

Uniqueness is guarded with increasing desperation. An Austrian company which invented a new method of making rubber and plastic seals did not take out a patent because it feared competitors would find a way round it. Instead they manufactured in carefully constructed secrecy. Their employees were not allowed to learn both the chemical and production sides of their process. For the time being, the process remains secret and unique.

No matter what the business, even Motivity's cleverly invented niche, uniqueness does not last long. Indeed, history suggests that uniqueness is rarely achieved.

At the leading edge of research there are often groups of people spread throughout the world trying to achieve the same or similar objectives. Nobel prize winners, for example, tend to be in teams competing for a specific goal. The winners reach the goal first – the others quickly learn from the winning solution and move inexorably on.

In business, the race to get products to market takes on a

similar pattern. Scientists from a number of multinational corporations are likely to be trying simultaneously to discover the new wonder drug. One will come up with its solution before the others. The rest will then counter with several versions of the same basic idea and, over time, a winner will emerge.

Unfortunately, the term 'winner' is now inappropriate and counter productive. As Philip Sadler and Keith Milmer argue in their book, *The Talent Intensive Organisation*:

> *All knowledge, sooner or later, becomes obsolete, or freely available, and thus ceases to be the basis for a lasting competitive advantage. It is not the stock of a company's (or a nation's) knowledge which provides a competitive advantage, it is the capacity to innovate, to develop new knowledge, that matters . . . Talent is the only remaining scarce resource.[22]*

In *Collaborating to Compete*, McKinsey consultants Joel Bleeke and David Ernst argue:

> *For most global businesses, the days of flat-out, predatory competiton are over. The traditional drive to pit one company against the rest of an industry; to pit supplier against supplier, distributor against distributor, on and on through every aspect of a business, no longer guarantees the lowest cost, best products or services, or highest profits for winners of this Darwinian game. In fact, the exact opposite is true.[23]*

Competitiveness is no longer solely about markets and niches, winners and losers. It is about people. There is no final solution, only ones which are current (and their life expectancy is shortening by the year). The key, therefore, is in recognising that strategy must take this into account, be continually enhanced by new ideas and optimise human resources at every turn.

There are some signs that organisations now realise that business is no longer simply a matter of achieving victory over some imagined adversary. There is, for example, increased use of partnership – between companies and with customers and suppliers. This realisation has led drug companies to pool their resources in the quest to develop certain drugs. On a single day in 1993, Warner-Lambert of the US announced a global joint venture with the UK company Wellcome and a strategic alliance with Glaxo Holdings, Europe's biggest drugs company, to market its prescription drugs. Such announcements are now commonplace. The search for a new anti-AIDs drug led to sixteen leading companies bringing their research teams together. This was not a humanitarian gesture, but commercial recognition that this is the best way of making money in this area.

This trend is also fuelled by the globalisation of markets. In global markets, companies have to be global in reach. For many, working alone, this is simply impossible. They have to seek out new avenues of international partnership and collaboration. It is a challenge that governments are also wrestling with. Increasingly, they too are facing global problems – such as AIDs – which the traditional structures are too inflexible or geographically limited to deal with.

The globalisation of markets is not the only challenge. The rapidity of change in many markets now means that instead of a gradual process, companies are having to come to terms with revolution. They have to re-define the demands of their market and their role within it.

Historically, strategists have not had to concern themselves with continual re-definition. In a few businesses, however, the process appears established. In the fashion industry there is the public impression of originality. The annual launches of new lines remorsely press home the message of striking originality. Every year the market is re-defined.

In other businesses manufacturers put the word '*New*' on a pack and watch as sales routinely rise by 10 per cent. Fashion models do not display anything so coarse as a sticker guaranteeing originality. They don't have to – everyone knows that fashions come in cycles and there is nothing new on the catwalk to display, but the veneer of progress sustains an entire industry.

If success is no longer a matter of uniqueness and originality, it is a question of finding the context in which a product or service can succeed. In psychological-speak, businesses now need to discover synchronicity – a moment in time when there are parallel objectives or a coincidence of intent.

It is, to a large extent, a question of putting a new meaning to old ideas. There is, for example, nothing original in the much recorded story of Ray Kroc and McDonalds. The hamburger is an established product and was so when Kroc came upon it. His innovation was to standardise its delivery across the country and present it in a consistently clean and welcoming environment. Success was built on his belief that he could change the world view of hamburgers. The product remained quintessentially the same, the context did not. Kroc's gold was a matter of synchronicity – the timing was right and his solutions fitted the new environment.

The UK retail chain, Sainsbury's is another example of a company which is continually changing the context of its business. It brings in new products – obscure fruits from South America which no one really knows what to do with. It gives people what they dream they might want. Slowly, each range catches on or fades away. People believe that shopping at Sainsbury's is a little bit more adventurous than it actually is.

Many other markets are being subtly re-defined. McDonalds has had to respond to increasing health consciousness. Volvo sought to replace the car industry's fascination with sex and speed and re-defined the market in terms of safety. Advertisers now know that the emphasis of a car's safety feature will often be recalled by the public as a Volvo feature – even if it was advertised by another manufacturer.

A more basic re-definition of the market was achieved by Swatch. It created a mass market by marketing watches as fashion accessories rather than mere time pieces.

In the toy business, Lego has continually re-defined its product to alter the context of the business. While it has changed, others such as Meccano have stood still.

To some extent, companies and managers are having to become used to accepting less. Newness and uniqueness is exciting, but in the 1990s not necessarily the best route to individual and corporate success. Instead of continually re-inventing the wheel, companies will be forced to spend more time honing and perfecting the wheel they have already created. Instead of re-definition, the onus will be on refinement. In the luxury hotel business, for example, the trend over recent years has been for hotels to add more and more trinkets and treats. 'During the 1980s hoteliers kept competing with each other with such things as large and expensive designer soaps, shampoos, lotions and presents of all types. As a result some hotel bathrooms looked like a beauty counter,' says Ramon Pajares, general manager of London's Inn on the Park.[24] Now, the emphasis is on returning to basics – the hotels have realised that customers want better service rather than chocolates under their pillows. The Inn on the Park now offers an overnight shoe cleaning service rather than peripheral gifts.

For managers the new importance of synchronicity opens appalling spectres of confusion and compromise. It demands that managerial skills be highly sophisticated.

In this environment managers are dealing with:

- More demanding consumers than ever before. Managers must be in-tune with their needs and the subtlest of variations between different consumer groups.
- Elusive markets which emerge and disappear more quickly. Managers have to understand their markets deeply and intuitively.
- Partnership is growing more important. Instead of an adversarial approach, organisations need to work together – and with customers and suppliers – to achieve mutuality.
- No winners. Managers and organisations have to come to terms with the fact that there are no winners – only participants and, even then, participation is never guaranteed.
- New measurements of success. The old measures of success have been drastically realigned. They are now far reaching, including issues such as environmental and ethical performance, as well as traditional financial indicators.
- Farewell to originality. Originality is dead, replaced by creativity (the ability to create new approaches to old situations) and a relentless search for concensus.

HOW HIGH PERFORMERS MAKE INTUITION WORK

As the credits roll on the satirical television programme, *Spitting Image*, acknowledgement is made to the programme's inspiration – a lunchtime conversation. A highly successful and innovative business has emerged not from a board room, but a restaurant.

This is not how we imagine strategies for success being created. Yet, other success stories are similarly based on inspiration and intuition rather than august board room meetings with the lingering smoke of the chairman's cigar wafting over data-wielding participants.

In a profile of newspaper proprietor Lord Rothermere, a newspaper observed: 'He has an almost Japanese fondness for strategy, though his concept of strategy has more to do with cunning and predicting what his competitors might do, than research-led analysis.'[25]

Rothermere, it seems, had built his empire on his knowledge of the market, the major players and shrewd judgement. The fact that he does not spend his time gathering pages of data does not strike us as unduly odd. We know that major decisions in both our business and personal lives are often based on mysterious hunches. 'I am a rational man but the biggest decisions you take on instinct,' observed Osvaldo Ardilles on deciding to become Tottenham Hotspur manager.[26] Such intuitive powers are a strong force and highly persuasive, pushing logical obstacles to one side, and defying reason. 'I am intuitive and go with gut feeling. If something feels right I don't understand where it's taking me but it just feels right,' observed John Charles.

The beauty of strategy is that the most intuitive, spontaneous and illogical decisions can be made to make sense. Retrospective strategy is a common feature in annual reports. If a ball-bearing manufacturer suddenly buys a distillery it is explained by the company's diversification strategy and there is, no doubt, much talk of synergy. This impresses institutional investors and analysts. If the chief executive explained that he simply had a hunch that the distillery was a good idea, commentators would be less impressed – even if that was the unvarnished truth.

Intuition almost became respectable in the 1980s. Yes, annual reports continued to invent neat strategic interpretations of history, but observers had a lot more time for the intuitive decision – if it worked.

The sudden discovery of intuition and its development to near respectability was, in part, a reaction against the data-driven strategist of the 1960s and 1970s. The image of the dashing entrepreneur was based in part on a dislike of the stereotypically dull accountant-manager. Who needed analytical tools and flow charts when running businesses was instinctive? People began to believe that there was indeed an entrepreneurial spirit waiting to emerge from within.

Prior to this rush of blood (perhaps inspired by the fact that it is easier to run a business during a relative boom time) intuition had a bad press. It was portrayed as a rare gift, hardly to be trusted in the day-to-day hurly burly of management.

The trouble is that intuition cannot be measured and is difficult to explain. Investors are unlikely to be impressed by a business plan based on a mysterious hunch which tells you there is a gap in the market. Shareholders would undoubtedly feel a little suspicious if the chief executive admitted that the stunning strategy came to him in the bath.

But, for many managers, intuition (gut feeling, hunch or instinct) is a critical part of their job. Stock Exchange traders don't have the time to call a meeting before they sell or buy at a certain rate; they back their intuition.

Intuition is a vital element of personnel selection – something the high performers pay careful attention to. 'As recruitment consultants we need to base our decisions on objective data,' says Helen Pitcher, director of Cedar International. 'But managers are eventually selected because of intuitive judgement. All the candidates can do the job, but for some reason you feel you can work better with x than with y. It is personal chemistry and, to some extent, prejudice.'[27]

Making the wrong intuitive decision can prove extremely costly. It is, says Helen Pitcher, an area where women are better equipped than their male counterparts. 'Women are more at home admitting they're not sure, but have a feeling that someone is more suited to the job. Men tend to come to hard and fast judgements.'

Intuition is a core skill of many managers – though it is not necessarily recognised as such by the managers or those they work with. 'Intuition is all about flexibility – being tuned into what's going on and being prepared to change direction,' says Robert Drummond, chairman of Grosvenor Venture Managers. By its very nature, venture capital relies on hunches and intuitive feelings on whether a business is likely to succeed or fail.

According to Robert Drummond, it is not simply a question of backing winners. 'It is no good following rigid rules in business. Successful people not only make the right decisions, they have an intuitive grasp of timing. Being a venture capitalist is all about being opportunistic; using your intuition to identify changes in society and invest in areas which meet new needs.'[28]

Some argue that intuition comes with experience. Managers begin to take decisions intuitively when they have made similar decisions before and can draw on a vast amount of corporate know-how. 'Very senior managers often appear to operate intuitively,' says psychologist Robert Sharrock of IARC-Ashridge. 'They don't use the usual buzz-words or adhere to textbook models of management. It is like mastering a skill or craft – putting it into practice becomes automatic. Though it may not seem so, a lot of intuition is, in fact, highly skilled.' Less experienced, younger managers are, therefore, unlikely to have the necessary intuitive skill to make instant decisions. 'For managers who have a lot of experience and intelligence, intuitive judgements are probably reliable. Others need to be extremely cautious,' warns Robert Sharrock.[29]

With increasing emphasis on the speed of decision-making, intuition is likely to become more and more important. 'Uncertainty breeds intuition,' argues Colin Carnall of Henley Management College. 'Things now happen so fast managers rarely have all the information they might need. They have to rely on their intuition if they are to seize the opportunity.'

Professor Carnall believes that intuitive managers, willing to back their judgement with immediate action, are the people who get to the top. 'Senior managers are not necessarily the most intelligent. Usually they are pragmatic and flexible, able to make intuitive decisions quickly and reliably rather than waiting for exhaustive analysis befor they make a move.'[30]

In the 1990s intuition is gaining greater credence in the hurly burly of day-to-day management. Brainstorming, now an acceptable activity, is little more than an attempt to extract intuitive responses. Increasingly, intuition is also seen as a skill which can be learned. 'Intuition is the ability to learn from experience,' says Robert Drummond. 'Companies need intuitive people – not necessarily at the very top of the organisation.' Indeed some organisations, such as 3M, have built their reputation on encouraging people throughout the company to follow their intuition. They recognise that, in the end, all the market research in the world cannot assure success. Business is not necessarily logical. If it were, well-constructed strategies would always succeed.

Intuition often provides the vital spark to ignite a good idea. The intuitive manager puts things together in a way that creates paradoxes and opportunities.

For the high performers, intuition was an accepted, integral part of their management style. As with key simplicities, they appeared acutely aware of when to follow intuitive sparks. They never dismissed their intuitive responses to situations – neither did they blindly follow them, no matter what. Instead, they recognised what their intuition told them and sought out confirmation that it was the right thing to do. Only then did they act.

Table 4.2

Intuitive high performers	*Analytical rationalists*
Are able to take decisions quickly and confidently.	Believe in steady progress to decision-making.
Use data sparingly and only when necessary.	Seek supportive data at every stage.
Recognise intuition as a skill.	Deny intuition.
Accept and encourage ideas.	Demand that ideas have an obvious use.
Act on intuitive judgements.	Question all judgements.
Accept no right or wrong method.	Insist that there is a right method.

THE LEADER AS RESOURCE

In *The Tao of Leadership* by John Heider there is one of those neat, aphoristic observations which appear to simplify management: 'The wise leader does not push to make things happen but allows the process to unfold on its own. The leader knows that constant interventions will block the group's process.'[31]

In reality, although the leader is probably aware that constant interventions are unhelpful, it is difficult to resist. You want your expertise to be utilised constantly. This is commonly seen as the way experienced managers add value. Often, however, they are simply adding to the complexity. Perhaps, more helpful is the American President's remark: 'As a leader you can get anything done in life if you don't mind who gets the credit.'

The high performers do not appear to be concerned with who gets the credit. Nor are they caught in a hierarchical straitjacket. They are willing to take part as an equal in group discussions and are anxious that their colleagues regard them as a resource, a conduit to more information, or a problem-solver.

This is usually not a matter of providing constant guidance which runs the risk of being intrusive. Instead, the manager channels people's energy in the right direction, sometimes surreptitiously, more obviously when it is required.

Robert Dunn explained how he went about fulfilling this role, helping others to play their part in meeting objectives: 'A philosopher once said that the best work is done by the people if they think they've done it themselves. They feel a sense of achievement if they've done it. You may have just guided them occasionally or structured it at the beginning, coached them or just said "you are good enough, do it your way".' Like many of the other building blocks and keys to high performance, this is a question of confidence and judgement.

Others place 'open door' style management as the key to

their approach. This is how Robert Dunn went on to explain his philosophy:

'I suppose my unorthodox style is that people don't actually work for me, they work with me and I work with them. That's how I actually believe I can get the best performance out of individuals. You have to give them a mixture of collective direction so they can see how all the parts come together. More importantly, I think you have to give them time. I like to give my people time so they won't find me rushing out of the door at 5 pm. If they want to talk to me, we sit there and we take what time it needs. I think it is important to give them time and I think it is about treating them on a level.

'I don't believe you get respect by demanding it. They'll respect you because you are prepared to help them when they need help, are prepared to give them encouragement when appropriate and also constructive criticism when needed. That's something else that works for me, particularly when you are developing people. They have to see the relevance of the things you want changed to still feel that they are running the project, but that they have liaised or consulted with you.'

Undoubtedly, this approach is something which works successfully for Robert. It is something he feels comfortable with. But, it is also clear that it does not occur casually. He recognises that it is 'unorthodox', a way of working which he can develop and utilise in a way that makes his management style appear to be highly individualistic rather than mechanistic. It is something he has thought about and cultivated.

Others earn respect by carrying out apparently menial tasks which emphasise where their preoccupations lie. Tinkering with the minutiae of corporate activity can, however, be a dangerous habit and is one many managers fall into. Don Lord spends time contacting customers who have complained. He believes, in a small way it is an important example.

> *'It has a wonderful effect. They think it's tremendous that I've taken the trouble to talk to them about their complaint. I can't do it every day because I don't have the time, but it has tremendous value. Similarly, if one of my staff says they were talking to someone who was complaining about something and they're going to stop the newspaper, I'll ring them. If I'm out of touch with why customers are discontent, I am unable to make changes which will keep them there as customers.'*

Talking to customers is regarded by Don as an important ingredient in, what he calls, 'getting people on your side'.

> *'If they can see the good sense in what you're doing they support it. It is not a question of looking at the hierarchy and then selecting them. It's a question of picking out opinion-formers from among the teams and helping them to understand the value of what you're doing. You don't just do that with your own department, you do it to other departments as well. It is a very good investment of time. It is what is fashionably called networking. I didn't realise I did a certain amount of networking – but I realise now, it is the way to get things through.'*

Don sees himself as a channeller of ideas, a provider of direction. He is very good at selecting the right people to persuade and is then confident enough to step back and watch the process unfold before him. Networking is mentioned casually, something he does unconsciously, yet is central to his management style and which has helped him guide the company through a period of radical change.

As a resource, the high performers preferred face-to-face contact. Some, like Ken Lawrie, think of everything in terms of people. Abrupt and direct, he thrives on personal contact. Crucially, he knows that people respond to him when they are face to face and that he is more effective in such situations. Despite his reputation for tough talking he is shy and reticent during larger meetings. He made a visit to a South American subsidiary which he described to us. 'I first listen to what people have to say. I recognise they have pride in what they're doing. I then suggest what builds on what they already do.' His approach was diplomatic, putting faith in evolution. He did not wish to appear to undermine confidence or seem to have jetted in with a manifesto. He wanted to guide rather than rule.

When visiting a Belgian manager, he took another approach. He realised that the manager was new in the job and inexperienced, as well as a little unwilling to toe the corporate line. Ken identified this and made sure he spoke alone to the manager so he could learn more about him – he spent three hours talking to him to clarify what they were both trying to achieve.

Managers who succeed in the personal – as opposed to personnel – side of management are likely to have learned to be adaptable to other styles. Ken ran a plantation in his twenties and was forced to accept a completely foreign approach to management and working. He learned to listen, communicate and respond. Despite often having vehement opinions, he does not impose them or his behaviour on other people. Instead, he is a constant counter balance, a kind of devil's advocate.

John Michaels is similarly capable of switching styles to fit the particular needs of a situation. At some meetings he sits back, content to listen rather than be an active contributor. At other times he is capable of leading from the front, dramatically arguing his case before large gatherings of sceptical managers.

There is another important facet to this. The personal
touch from senior managers does not always work. Managing
by walking about sounds like a good idea – and any manager
worth his or her salt is already doing it quite naturally – but it
can look very forced – the firm handshake at the office party;
the sudden concern for an employee's family. Managers also
often talk about their open-door policy as if this grants
managers instant and constant access. They might not
mention that managers have to get past the indomitable and
protective personal assistant or the fact that the office is
nearly always empty.

The enthusiasm for personal contact, however vacuous
and useless, is part of the widely held belief in personal
charisma. Charisma may well work for many business
leaders, but it cannot be emulated. Growing a beard and
wearing colourful jumpers rather than staid suits does not
transform you into a Richard Branson.

While the high performers were not charismatic – certainly
not in the colourful knitwear sense – some built their
approach around the belief that their very presence is re-
assurring and helpful. It often appears to be.

Catrina Carlberg puts a huge reliance on her people. She
appears to have perfected the trick of arriving, finding people
harried or perplexed and then acting as a catalyst as they sort
it out. She is content to sit in the background, acting as a
prompt rather than an instantaneous problem-solver. This
freewheeling, almost presidential, role is one which can work
only if the individual has the respect of their colleagues to an
unprecedented degree.

Generally, the high performers had outgrown the notion of
the individualistic leader, striving to lead by impressive
example. Instead, they regarded leadership as a question of

drawing people together and pulling disparate parts of the organisation together in a way that made individuals and the organisation more effective. The leader, as a resource:

- adds value as a coach, mentor and problem-solver rather than as a source of interference;
- allows people to accept credit for success . . . and responsibility for failure;
- considers, evaluates and enhances their own leadership role on a continuous basis;
- follows no rigid or orthodox role models, preferring to nurture their own unique leadership style;
- does not indulge in leadership by continual practical example (doing people's jobs for them) or personality cult (a benign casual-wear dictatorship);
- realises that leadership is as much to with the organisation as the individual;
- continually invests time in people – colleagues, employees, suppliers and customers;
- manages on a personal, often face-to-face, basis continually and naturally.

USING OBSESSION

'The only way to enjoy life is to work. Work is much more fun than fun.' We have all met business people who believe Noel Coward's adage to be true. To them, there is no dividing line between work and pleasure. They might be Eurobond dealers who work twelve-hour days fuelled by a concoction of adrenalin, coffee and pure fear; factory managers who stay long after everyone has left to pore over the day's work; sales managers who spend hour after hour in their cars listening to tapes teaching them how to be more successful. For them management has become much more than work or fun. It has become an obsession.

In business, obsessiveness is not a curious foible. Often it is not even regarded as strange or unhealthy. In fact, some see it as a good thing. People don't lose their jobs for being workaholics or devoting every moment of their lives to meeting sales targets. In fact, the number of hours they spend at work is often assumed to be a reliable measure of how efficient and committed they actually are.

Stupendous levels of commitment were highly fashionable in the 1980s. The 1990s, however, seem to have brought some realisation that success is not necessarily attributable to the number of hours worked. As pressures on managers mount, the solution of trying harder will no longer suffice.

Even so, managers persist in the belief that the more hours they work the better the quality of their work. It is an ethic not only prelavent in the West. In Japan it is encouraged from an early age through intense educational competition.

If they are forced to justify why they spend every waking hour thinking about work, the obsessive might point to the plethora of like-minded role models. There are a great many to choose from. Obsession is a recurring theme in virtually every artistic field. Films are full of obsessives who really should be in therapeutic clinics. Indiana Jones is obsessive; Westerns are usually built around someone's obsession with 'cleaning up the town'; what else can explain Rocky's determination or Gordon Ghecko's behaviour in *Wall Street*?

The lure of obsession is seen elsewhere. The actor Alan Bates has said: 'Everyone who's any good is obsessive.'

Athletes and sports people are particularly prone to obsessiveness. Their excuse is that their particular skill is likely to disappear rapidly with age. Historians also tend to elevate obsessives to star status – we all know, for example, that Henry VIII was obsessed with fathering a son and that Napoleon was obsessed with conquering Russia. Though history converts obsession into a positive attribute it doesn't have to live with the obsessives. Literary blockbusters usually have obsessive leading men and women – from Hamlet to Scarlett O'Hara. There is even a perfume called 'Obsession', suggesting that, at the very least, the obsessive is likely to smell nice.

Within business, obsessive managers can point to a lengthy list of like-minded individuals who reached the top. George Davies, the businessman behind the rapid growth of the UK retail chain, Next, started work before eight in the morning and often left the office at eleven at night. Not only was he obsessed, his employees were. 'At times I think we were rather like a religious sect. Our staff would go home and talk about Next,' he observes in his autobiography.[32]

Profiles of business people inevitably uncover obsessive characteristics. A friend of the publisher Tim Hely Hutchinson says of him: 'He's a driven man. He's got one overwhelming interest in life and that is to build the business.'[33]

There are many other similar examples. Ray Kroc used to pick up litter from car parks and was discovered one Saturday morning cleaning the muck out of the holes on a mop bucket with a tooth brush. The crew handbook which all McDonalds workers receive lists strict dress codes based on hygiene considerations and is prefaced by the words 'Cleanliness is like a magnet drawing customers to McDonalds'.

Some recount more extreme stories. Victor Kiam says: 'Business is a game and eight hours don't afford you enough time to score the deciding run.' As a youthful, but obsessed, salesman, Kiam stalked the United States seeking out every advantage possible. 'When a snowstorm hit my region it wasn't an obstacle; it was an opportunity! It was amazing how receptive a buyer could be when the snow outside his door was waist deep and climbing, and you were the only friendly face he had seen all day,' he later reflected.[34]

The belief is that obsession inspires commitment and energises previously inert managers. 'I believe if someone comes to work for me I pay them well, but I expect them to give their absolute and I never believe you should tell people to do things. You should ask them and they should expect to come in early every morning and go home late at night and just work and work for me because they enjoy doing it,' says Richard Webster.

If obsessive managers took a step back it would be easy for them to recognise the unhealthy side of the obsession. It dominates their life to the detriment of family, friends and fun. At work it may cloud their judgement – often they are so obsessed they are incapable of being objective.

Working for an obsessive boss poses unique problems and is rarely compatible with job security. Interestingly, Richard Webster attempts to get round this by employing people with a similar approach to his own.

'Obsession is where commonsense bites the dust,' says a manager who has worked for two bosses he identifies as obsessive. 'I did not go along with the obsession so I was quickly shown the door.

'But the people I worked with carried on working obsessive numbers of hours and did not question the boss's demanding habits. To the obsessive boss no-one else's world matters. If you point out, as I did, that their decisions are not rational but based on obsessive prejudice, you can guarantee fireworks.'

The dividing line between commitment (healthy and outward looking) and obsession (unhealthy and inward looking) is a thin one. It is a precarious balancing act.

Among the high performers, there were clear signs of obsessive behaviour. They worked long hours and appeared extraordinarily committed to achieving their goals. John Charles said:

Lots of people have said to me that I analyse things to death. I intuitively believe that you can go on and on peeling into problems. It's like an onion and you'll never reach the centre. There isn't a solid centre, it's just layers so that when you peel away the last layer all you are left with is space, it's not like there's a nut. So to get to the heart of the problem you've got to go on asking yourself and you've got to go on peeling. Now the trouble is I don't usually have the time and I don't have the forum or the environment to enable me to do that.

Given the opportunity, John would undoubtedly have developed his obsessive craving for analysis. But, the momentum continually generated by his ideas acts as a counter to this. Passionate about ideas, he has to move on.

'The work of a lot of senior executives demands that they are extraordinarily focused and thorough in what they do,' says Robert Sharrock of IARC-Ashridge. 'But paradoxically they cannot afford to be narrow in their outlook. Companies need a combination of extremely focused managers and ones with more of an entrepreneurial outlook taking in the broader picture.'[35]

Having sailed across the Atlantic, Jonathan Jeffes knows a

thing or two about obsession. Now managing director of Westward Training and Development, he believes that companies are becoming better at identifying obsessives, whether they are empire-builders or obsessively competitive, and re-directing their energy.

'Managers are often obsessed with the wrong thing – how many hours they work on a particular task,' he says. 'Obsession, like anything else, needs to be channelled in the right direction. If it isn't, you end up with managers doing their own thing for the own ends rather than working as a team.'[36]

Bob Kaplan of the US Center for Creative Leadership prefers not to use the word obsessive, with its negative connotations. In his book *Beyond Ambition*, Kaplan came up with the word 'expansive' to sum up the obsessive striving of many managers.

> *Executives desire a sense not merely of adequacy but of high personal worth, and they seek it not by doing an acceptable job but by doing an exceptional job. Expansive executives see themselves, perhaps unconsciously, as heroes. Like heroes, they want to execute some masterstroke, or accomplish prodigious amounts of work, or adhere to the highest standards.'[37]*

The positive side of obsession does not only lie in seeking to achieve the highest possible standards. 'If you are not obsessed with your idea there is no point in starting a business,' says Tim Scott of the Business Founder's Bureau. 'But if you are to overcome the myriad of obstacles ahead, establish credibility and succeed, you have to temper your obsession with reality. Obsessives need a touchstone – often their partner – to bring them back to earth. Otherwise they end up being blind to many of the pitfalls.'[38]

For the self-employed obsession is, paradoxically, often

essential. Again, the balance is delicate. Bank managers are likely to be more reticent in lending money to an obsessed zealot with a distant gleam in his eye than to someone who is obsessed with achieving quality products at competitive prices.

It should also be said that obsession is not simply an individualistic phenonemon. Corporately, obsession can lead to costly errors. IBM's obsession with mainframes has probably had a significant impact on its competitive advantage in other areas of computing.

Obsession is a potent force which needs to be harnessed to the organisational good rather than being allowed to gather pace by itself. Managers, for example, expend huge amounts of energy in obsessive search of promotions and engaging in corporate politics. If this energy was set free, and channelled, a potentially enormous corporate and individual resource would be unleashed. Managing obsession successfully involves:

- recognising obsessive qualities in yourself and channelling and directing them to the organisational good;
- recognising obsessive qualities in others and focusing their energies where most effective;
- identifying the divide between healthy and unhealthy obsession (ensuring, for example, that TQM (total quality management) does not develop into obsessive form-filling);
- questioning corporate assumptions and long-held obsessions whether they be with particular people, products, strategies or markets;
- using obsession as an inspirational example. Ray Kroc's diligence is a story which has entered into corporate

folklore and, more importantly, the McDonald's culture.

'Obsession doesn't guarantee success. On the other hand a lack of obsession does guarantee failure,' observes Tom Peters in his latest blockbuster, *Liberation Management*.[39] Obsession is a managerial necessity.

GETTING THE MESSAGE ACROSS

Every hour over 100 million telephone calls are made using 300 million lines across the world. It is predicted that this figure will treble by the year 2000. 'Those who are most plugged into this global conversation stand to gain the most from it,' predicted Alan Webber in a recent *Harvard Business Review* article. 'Conversations are the way knowledge workers discover what they know, share it with their colleagues and in the process create new knowledge for the organisation.'[40]

In the technological age, clear and effective communication is vital. Among the high performers sustaining high quality communication at all times was regarded as a vital part of their job. They realised that without clear communication good ideas disappear into the corporate ether.

Keeping it simple

The supply of information and opinions the managers received was incredibly complex. Karl-Heinz Muller received a constant stream of letters, calls and faxes from his client, partners, colleagues and his own company. Yet, he and the other managers were able to make sense of it and extract the important details from the vast bulk of paper and input from a wide variety of sources. No matter what, they kept communication as simple as possible. It is an approach shared by many successful companies.

One major organisation uses codenames for its projects. Not all of them are highly sensitive, so there is no real need for secrecy. But, managers find that using a codename acts as shorthand – people instantly understand what they are talking about.

'If we can simplify something we will. If we can make it simple we can communicate it easily to our people and people can understand, champion it and endeavour to take an active part in the programme,' observed John Cahill when chief executive of BTR.[41] With operations across the world, thousands of employees and contracts worth hundreds of millions of pounds, BTR still manages to succeed with what most would regard a skeletal central staff. Key to this is its insistence that managers communicate simply with accurate and pithy résumés rather than exhaustive analyses.

The high performers also put their faith in simplicity. Richard Webster, chairman of a large engineering company, advocates verbal communication to achieve greater openness and honesty among his managers.

The people who don't fit in with the team and cause problems tend to be the type who write letters. I mean if my directors write to each other they get in trouble because why should you ever want to write to someone in the same building as you? What you do is walk into their office and say, 'What the hell are you doing? Explain it to me.' You don't write something sarcastic. The people who do are normally quite weak. I want them to go in and say, 'Look we've got a problem, what the hell are you doing that for?'

Brevity was much championed. Ken Lawrie summed up preparing a budget: 'It's really just a matter of presenting a very complex issue as simply as possible and then discovering when you present it simply that you don't like the answer yourself.'

He is a master of simple and direct communication and described his ambitions for the company in a typically simplistic image. His 'three egg model' was something he often mentioned. It did not demand a great deal of knowledge to understand. 'Basically, we are a small egg at the moment. We want to be a big egg. Along the way we may need to become an intermediately sized egg,' he said. Though he was used to dealing with large sums of money and a highly complex business, he explained it all in terms of eggs. It was simplistic – but people understood.

Simplicity and brevity demonstrated a great faith in directness. The managers did not want to spend time messing around. If something needed communicating, they went ahead and did so. As many worked in international businesses, this wasn't always very easy.

Even so, face-to-face meetings and contact were still regarded as crucial.

'I'm a great believer in face-to-face personal things, sort of talking it through, so I spend a lot of time travelling around the country. I'm not a believer in sending out great long memos. Instead, I think that to win confidence and communicate properly you need to talk it through with people, preferably at ground floor level,' said one manager. Other high performers travelled extensively to ensure that they actually met people rather than relying on telephones and faxes.

David Andrews sold his strategic review by travelling to

each of the company's divisions throughout the world and explaining it to them. They felt involved, and slightly flattered that he had gone to some lengths to meet them.

Ken Lawrie talked to as many people as possible to hear their views on the company's strategy and give them his own – 'I spend time talking to everyone about the implications of the strategy,' he said.

Catrina Carlberg saw her travelling as an important opportunity for face-to-face discussions. Others agreed that talking on a plane was a good way of covering issues which might have normally been left untouched and of opening people up to share their fears and aspirations.

Language to inspire

Often language is the jailer of our ambitions and potential. If we can't articulate our strategy in terms which inspire others what chance have they of understanding or participating? As Robert Haas, chairman and chief executive of Levi Strauss, says:

> *A strategy is no good if people don't fundamentally believe in it. We had a strategy in the late 1970s and early 1980s that emphasised diversification. We acquired companies, created new brands, and applied our traditional brand to different kinds of apparel. Our people did what they were asked to do, but the problem was, they didn't believe in it.*[42]

Belief makes things possible; lack of understanding breeds apathy and contempt.

Part of the problem is that the language of management often operates as more of an exclusion zone than as a means of clarifying issues and messages. It is deeply bedded in a coded argot of bastardisations, adaptations, abbreviations and jargon.

Although often tortuous, the language of management is based on a number of key images and analogies. Managers routinely extract images from: mechanics; medicine; sports and the military. The attractions are usually straightforward.

- *Mechanics*: comparisons with machinery suggest that even the smallest cog has a part to play. Although this may be motivational, the corollary is that any mistake or malfunction can also be traced back to an identifiable cog or employee. The current management buzz-word, re-engineering, is bound up with this particularly robotic image.
- *Medicine*: the body-corporate is often talked of as an ailing individual in need of managerial medicine. Organisational development literature, for example, is peppered with talk of transforming organisations from 'unhealthy' to 'healthy' states. However, we all know that certain illnesses can prove fatal.
- *Sports*: analogies with sports come in a vast variety of forms. These have the advantage that they are easily understood and usually come with strong mental images of winning and endurance. They do, however, have a short life – sporting heroes come and go – and the analogies cannot usually be pushed too far before becoming inappropriate or ineffective.
- *Military*: senior managers have traditionally mined a rich vein of military imagery. With the end of the Cold War, these may no longer be applicable. The attraction is often that military lines of command appear crystal clear and the onus is on action and ultimate victory.

Until the 1940s strategy was seen as the preserve of the

military. The Oxford English Dictionary continues this, defining strategy as 'the art of a commander-in-chief'. Strategy remains rooted in a military context, although the language has changed with time. 'Strategy is the deployment of one's resources in a manner which is most likely to defeat the enemy, said General Ulysses Grant in 1860. Strategy is seeking and maintaining a sustainable advantage,' wrote Richard Rumelt in the 1980s.[43]

Management writer Robert Evered observes:

Initially strategies referred to the general in command of an army, later it came to mean the art of the general, which is to say the psychological and behavioural skills which he used. By the time of Pericles (450 BC) it came to mean managerial skill and by Alexander's time (330 BC) it referred to the skill of employing forces to overcome opposition and to create a unified system of global governance.[44]

As times have changed, so too has strategy and the language of management. The images managers use and are comfortable with have different sources and inspirations. As Charles Handy says in his book, *The Age of Unreason*:

One sign of the new sorts of organisation is a perceptible change in the language we use to talk about them. Organisations used to be perceived as gigantic pieces of engineering, with largely interchangeable human parts. We talked of their structures and their systems, of inputs and outputs, of control devices and of managing them, as if the whole was one large factory. Today the language is not that of engineering but of politics, with talk of cultures and networks, of teams and coalitions, of influence or power rather than control, of leadership not management.[45]

Images for high performance

Even so, much of today's managerial vocabulary owes a great deal to traditional imagery. While the concept of strategy started off in warfare, and has developed and changed quite considerably, the analogies we use for business structures do not seem to have changed quite so dramatically. We still talk about doing battle with the competition. We make comparisons between our organisations and machines and mechanical or electrical systems. These metaphors need to be updated. By raising language above clichéd imagery, managers can have a profound effect.

Management writers and thinkers are continually searching for new images and analogies to clarify the manager's role and the nature of organisations. No stone is left unturned. In *Powershift*, futurist Alvin Toffler creates a confusingly zoological image for the future.

> *The flex-firm concept does not imply structurelessness; it does suggest that a company in being reborn, may cease being a mule and turn into a team consisting of a tiger, a school of piranhas, a mini-mule or two, and who knows, maybe a swarm of information-sucking bees. The image underlines the point. The business of tomorrow may embody many different formats within a single frame. It may function as a kind of Noah's ark.*[46]

The high performers were acutely aware of the possibilities of language – although they did not indulge themselves to the extent Toffler envisages.

Describing how he encouraged his boss to change his views, John Charles explained how he used language:

> *I've used analogies and word pictures to take him gradually on-board. The mental image I have is of rolling countryside. The journey we've got to do is up and down those hills. But, if you go*

too far, you disappear out of sight into the next valley. And, if my boss can't see, he has no point of reference. So I can only take him a certain distance at each stage. I take him that distance then invite him to look back to where he's come from so he sees where his point of reference is. Then I say, 'Now look forward. You see the hill up there, that's the next point we are going to get to'. Then I take him on again. In between he's going to lose sight of me and what I am trying to achieve. But I've got to keep moving.

Other high performers had developed different metaphors to describe their own organisation. David Andrews said:

I view our business as a jewel, a diamond. We were going to look at the diamond from every possible direction, and in every direction another picture would emerge. We looked at the business against just about every variable that we could think of. It was a hell of an effort. But we were forcing people to look at the world, our place in it, the competition and our position relative to them.

It is also interesting to see metaphors developed by managers to explain their own role. One manager referred to his job as being like 'oil and lubricant, the things that make things happen'.

The fact that the managers use such a range of metaphors and analogies – diamonds, chess boards, hills and valleys – suggests that they are constantly on the look out for new ways of expression – modern and appropriate images to describe their role in the organisation and the organisation itself.

Images for the future

If we are to see strategy as growing from the bottom of the organisation then we must think in terms of organic metaphors. Could we conceive of an organisation as an organism, where a variety of different cells are meeting together? The process of forming and developing and discovering strategy may be akin to the RNA molecules combining to form new organisms. The gene bank of an organisation can get perilously thin when pressured by cost-cutting methods. At the opposite extreme, after a merger or takeover, too many genes will be present, some will be lost and much talent that could have been harnessed disappears to new external organisations.

Perhaps we can think of managers, indeed all staff, as strands of RNA or DNA concerned with reproducing the organisation every day and every year. If we think in those terms then the formulation of strategy becomes a process of identifying useful genes and trying to produce a better organism from the mix of genes that are currently available.

As Richard Dawkins has demonstrated in his book, *The Blind Watchmaker*,[47] the process of evolution in the real world depends enormously on mutation and the positive advantages to survival that some mutations bring. A similar process could easily be going on in our organisations without our conscious knowledge or approval. It requires a much bigger view to spot the process of natural selection working away in our organisations, especially when we believe we are having a major instrumental effect in making choices. Perhaps, as Dawkins has shown, our organisations are governed by a process and by rules which are outside our own control.

A scientific metaphor was used by Don Lord in an effort to explain his role in achieving and managing the change process.

Many of my journalists haven't moved very much at all. A lot of them have joined the company and stayed here most of their careers so it is a matter of selling them the need to change and for them to realise that the culture has to change. You don't just make one change and that's it – it's never right. It is a living organism, as is our society and, as society changes, we have continually to reflect those changes.

In changing times metaphors also must change. The new images are sometimes disturbing for managers reared on neat one-dimensional sports analogies about knockouts and being first past the post. In their book, *Collaborating to Compete*, Joel Bleeke and David Ernst come up with an original, but typically unsettling, metaphor for the organisation of the 1990s.

Global corporations of the future will be rather like amoebas. This single-celled aquatic animal is among the most ancient life-forms on earth. It gets all its nourishment directly from its environment through its permeable outer walls. These walls define the creature as distinct from its environment, but allows much of what is inside to flow out and much of what is outside to come in. The amoeba is always changing shape, taking and giving with the surroundings, yet it always retains its integrity as a unique creature.[48]

From being all-conquering armies, organisations have seemingly undergone reverse evolution to become shapeless sea creatures. Disturbing though they may be, such analogies and metaphors are a means by which managers can come to terms with the world around them. They are difficult to use successfully. Sometimes managers force their analogy on to the world when it has become patently inappropriate. It is a problem which constantly torments politicians who are anxious to create strong powerful images. The trouble is they often stick with them after they have passed their time or are misinterpreted.

High performers used analogies and metaphors sensitively

and effectively. They were flexible. One of the managers used different analogies for the size of the strategic picture facing him. He pitched his analogy at the level of the problem. They were also aware that although many metaphors have motivational value in that they can communicate something complex in an accessible way, they run the risk of being applied too regularly. Images were applied where appropriate rather than becoming over-used.

Table 4.3

High performance communications	Cloudy communications
Simplicity when ever possible.	Complex issues made more complex.
Jargon-free.	Preoccupied with using the latest jargon.
Brevity.	Verbosity.
Uses communications as knowledge-sharing.	Regards communications as a necessary evil.
Believes strategy implementation is reliant on clear communications.	Believes in strategy implementation.
Distills complex information easily.	Accumulates complex information.
Direct and personal.	Indirect and bureaucratic.
Uses simple images.	Regards simple images as simplistic.
Uses appropriate images.	Uses the same images repeatedly.
Identifies opportunities for communication continually.	Misses opportunities.

SELF-AWARENESS AND QUESTIONING

When managers were seen as omnipotent and dictatorial chief executives lurking in every board room, it was unthinkable to envision them questioning their outlook or behaviour. Among the managers we studied, however, there was an acute degree of self-awareness.

Sometimes this emerged in comments which appeared to border on arrogance. 'When I think of ideas it doesn't bother me if I can't pin them down. It doesn't concern me if I have no clear plan of action. I have a sort of inner reassurance that it will come out right,' said John Charles. Although, in fact, this appeared to be an honest assessment of how he managed.

Self-aware and confident of their ability, the managers believed they were good at what they did. Each manager's combination of experience was unique and unusually wide. This breadth of experience appeared to bolster their confidence in their ability to play the role assigned to them. The managers had found the style which best suited them and achieved change within their organisation. If the organisation changed, they were quite prepared to adopt styles to meet the new challenges. They played to the strengths which they judged to be appropriate to the circumstances.

But, just because you are able to play the piano, you don't *have* to play the piano. Some managers believe that they have to use all of their skills all of their time. High performers trusted their perception and their judgement in applying the right skills at the right time. They believed that if their perceptions led to certain conclusions then the conclusions would be obvious to others also.

Interestingly, the self-assurance inherent in the managers means that they didn't mention their own bosses very much. They sought to dictate their own role in the organisation and its parameters. 'When I took my job I said I wasn't prepared to be a corporate bean counter,' said David Andrews. Catrina Carlberg didn't mention her boss until she was asked repeatedly about her relationship with him.

David Andrews also put his boss in positions where he gave very public support to what David planned to do. This gave him the leverage and political power to achieve his objectives.

Although the current preoccupation in management theory is with managing your boss and managing upwards, the managers were content to negotiate their own space and then go ahead. As so often happened to John le Carré's Smiley, they were sent out on a task and found that the task expanded as they progressed. Often they encouraged their staff to do likewise. They recognised a general need for people to develop their own space and set their own limitations.

While bosses were not seen as an impediment to the high performers, there was a basic assumption that they would have broad support from them at all times. Karl-Heinz Muller proved himself particularly adept at calling his boss in at the right time to solve the right level of problem. He knows there is a point at which he can do no more to solve a problem. Equally, his boss knows that Karl-Heinz only calls him when the issue is important and his particular skills and authority are needed.

One manager we talked to sees himself as a risk-taker. Instead of guarding this as a key competitive weapon, he is anxious that others should follow suit:

If someone comes up with an idea and says to me 'Why don't we try doing this?' I will very often say okay, if you believe it will work then test it in your area then come back in six months and tell us if it worked. If it doesn't, it's alright – it's not the end of the world. It only costs us X thousand pounds so if it works maybe it's something we can develop throughout the company.

He does not regard taking risks as something he, as a senior manager, should regard as his sole preserve. It is something he wishes to encourage elsewhere in the organisation. Risk-taking is encouraged by him as a means of building up trust, empowering others and along the way, perhaps reaping the benefits for the business.

Asking questions

The high performers were aware of their limitations. They continually questioned themselves, their colleagues, sub-ordinates and superiors. They were persistent – 'You have to carry on and never take no for an answer. After all, it is always easy for people to say no,' said Catrina Carlberg.

Questioning is a central part of achieving change. 'In other companies the word is – don't rock the boat. Here we rock hell out of the boat. We don't know the factory's limits. We want it to change, to evolve,' a manager at US company Chaparral Steel told the *Sloan Management Review*.[49] The high performers felt similarly – they were never completely at ease with assumptions about what needed to be done or where things were leading.

Asking questions – and listening to the answers – is a very basic skill. Marketing guru Ted Levitt says:

You have to expose yourself to your environment and ask questions to develop your sensitivity and sensibility. 'I see things all the time. I go into factories, offices, stores and look out the window and just see things and ask 'Why?' Why are they doing that? Why are things this way and not that? You ask questions and pretty soon you come up with answers. When you begin to try to answer your own questions you become much more receptive to reading things which help you to answer questions. Seeing is one thing but perception requires cognitive effort and personal involvement. You bring something to what you see.[50]

And, unquestionably, asking questions doesn't necessarily make management any easier. On a personal level questioning can appear to express doubts about a colleague's ability or integrity. But, as Chris Argyris, has said: 'To question someone else's reasoning is not a sign of mistrust but a valuable opportunity for learning.'[51]

It is also true that the response may not be what you want to hear. The questioning manager must, as a result, learn to cope with and learn from unfavourable and unhelpful data. 'I think what really matters in getting ideas into action is being very clear on what you really want. I don't think we're always very honest about saying "I don't really know",' said Mike Sutcliffe, who infuriated all around him by his dedication to questioning basic assumptions.

The point about self-awareness and questioning appears simplistic. You can't teach self-awareness, although managers can acquire a broad range of experience to make them aware of a number of aspects of business. Nor can you teach people to be inquisitive. Yet, they are core skills without which it is difficult to see how any manager could function effectively.

MEASURING SUCCESS

'The only infallible criterion of wisdom to vulgar minds – success,' observed Edmund Burke. By Burke's criteria, there are a lot of vulgar minds in the business world.

Traditionally, our views of managerial success and failure

Table 4.4

High performers	Under achievers
Question decisions and assumptions at every turn.	Accept decisions and assumptions.
Show no fear of tackling their superiors.	Live in fear of insecurity and upsetting the *status quo*.
Acknowledge their skills and limitations.	Acknowledge their skills; deny their limitations.
Adapt to change.	Fear change.
Set the parameters of their functions.	Accept the parameters laid down by others.

have been tightly bound to financial performance. A successful chief executive oversees increases in profitability and/or share value. Despite performance-related pay and more flexible approaches to rewards and remuneration, little has happened to shake this basic premise.

In annual reports, chairman and chief executives routinely re-affirm their commitment to financial performance as their prime responsibility. Some express it in narrower terms than others. P&O chairman Lord Sterling has said: 'My first responsibility is to the shareholders of P&O and profit is what it is all about.'[52] Lord Hanson has said with equal forthrightness: 'The central tenet of my faith is that the shareholder is king.'[53]

The corollary of measuring managerial performance by financial success is that managerial success should be matched by financial reward. Yet, curiously, among the high performers there is little mention of financial motivation – whether individually or in terms of the organisation as a whole. None of the managers is, apparently, in a position to give up working for a living. Perhaps, money is looked upon as too crude a yardstick or motivatory carrot. It is, even so, conspicuously absent from their conversation.

Indeed, the high performers have a shifting flexible view of what constitutes success and failure, which matches their ever changing vision of the future. They do not use the language of targets and measured short-term gains. Instead, they recognise that change is likely to be incremental rather than revolutionary, that one step backwards might lead to a great leap forwards in the near future.

Success, they accept, is often immeasurable. After months of effort, David Andrews is able to philosophically observe: 'You would never be able to measure it [the changes] apart from hints that people are doing things a little differently.' This, however, was viewed by him as success.

Parallel to this is the perception that success is never stationary. It is not a matter of proceeding from A to B and then congratulating everyone while the competitors race by. 'The thing is you don't just make a single change and that's it . . . It's never right. It's a living organism, just like anything elese,' said Don Lord. Success, like everything else, is continually mutating and disappearing before your eyes. For other high performers success is seen in terms of ideas. John Charles remarked: 'If I could have one of those sparks of genius in my life it would be enough for me.'

The key for the majority is that success is inextricably linked to progress, action and direction; and involves a process of continuous improvement, personally and organisationally.

For some, success is practically based, all about getting jobs done and problems solved. 'The reward for all this is getting things to work, making them happen,' said Catrina

Carlberg, going on to talk about her personal motivation. 'It is important to decide how you reward yourself . . . It's not a question of money. I want to be able to have an impact on things. I don't want to be an important person myself – if I did, I would have stayed with a big company where there's more status.'

Interestingly, Catrina's comments show a common characteristic of the high performers. They are intent on improving themselves, making themselves more efficient managers, and helping their organisations towards long-term visions.

In parallel to viewing success as practical achievement, the high performers also tend to regard success and progress as one and the same. Karl-Heinz Muller said; 'I have a rough idea of where we stand day by day.' He is not really interested in knowing every single aspect of what is going on in the project so long as steady, monitored and measured progress is being made. In fact, progress and direction are seen as at least as important as the completion of immediate tasks. Progress is continually re-evaluated and what would amount to progress in the future gauged.

Looking back over the progress he has made in readying his organisation for radical change, John Michaels was honest enough to admit that his expectations had not always been met. Instead of expressing disappointment, he looked again at his view of the overall process: 'In some ways I am not sure we have made as much progress as I anticipated. I don't know if my perceptions of the process have changed – it is difficult to stand back – but it is now a lot more about looking to and contributing to the future.' Rather than seeking out scapegoats, John questions his own expectations.

The overall emphasis is on providing direction in uncertain times, clarifying complexity. The high performers regard their role as steering the corporate ship in the right general direction.

Explaining what he hoped to achieve from his strategic report, Ken Lawrie explained: 'What I try to produce is something people feel comfortable with and feel they want a role in. It might not deliver exactly what they want but they believe it's achievable, sensible, and well thought through.' It is a matter of giving a sense of direction rather than hard and fast targets.

Another aspect of this is that status, the perennial pre-occupation of managers, appears to be waning in significance. Catrina, typically of the high performers, has little time for her status within the company or society. Perhaps, as senior managers, it is easier for the high per-formers to be dismissive of what was once thought to be a prime motivator. But, we suspect, there is more to it than that.

Status, whether it be through seniority, company cars or other perks, is slowly disappearing as a yardstick of mana-gerial achievement. This has been largely caused by the new role of managers. The disappearance of hierarchies and the flattening of organisations encourages managers with a wide range of skills and brings an end to corporate career ladders – managers must expand their horizons horizontally rather than endlessly striving for vertical progression.

Managers who dream of a world filled with a succession of promotions are likely to be continually disappointed. A 1993 report by the Institute of Management[54] tracked the career development of over 800 managers from 1980 to 1992 It found that sideways or downwards moves among managers more than doubled in the last decade, rising from seven per 100 managers in 1980–1982 to nearly 15 per 100 managers in

1992.

'As the pace of change accelerates, the idea of a progressive career within stable organisational structures is increasingly threatened,' says the Institute of Management report. 'The structures which have traditionally supported rational long-term careers are being gradually replaced with more fluid organisations.' And it is people who are the most fluid of corporate resources. The report's co-author, Trudy Coe, says:

> *Managers need to look at their career differently. They have to see a sideways move as an opportunity to develop the broad portfolio of skills they now need. While in the past managers looked to organisations to shape their careers and skills for them, now the onus is on them. They need to be prepared for change and recognise its potential benefits rather than regarding it as a threat.*

Success as continuous development

Instead of being developed by the organisation, the emphasis is increasingly on the individual to be aware of their own development needs. In tandem with their company, they need continually to enhance their skills and learning.

The idea of managers enhancing their 'value' rather than their status is one which is gaining some recognition and is central to the obvious drive behind the high performers. As Bob Broadbent, business manager of ICL Consultancy and Technical Services, says:

> *I want to get away from the grading system where people get rises and promotion through seniority. I want our people to look on themselves as having a value in the marketplace and to grow that value; to be able to illustrate through their CVs (in an authentic*

way) that they have worked on significant projects and that they have achieved measurable results for our clients.[55]

While the notion of adding value is attractive, research by the Michael Lombardo at the US's Center for Creative Leadership[56] suggests that it may be a demanding target. According to Lombardo, managerial success is usually based on:

- track record;
- technical or business brilliance;
- outgoing charming personality;
- promotion in an acquisition of re-organisation;
- loyalty to management;
- ambition;
- leading subordinates.

Lombardo's work also suggests that managers who are successful relatively early in their careers often go through a process of 'derailment', where things go wrong and their flaws are exposed. Derailment, Lombardo believes, can be caused by:

- a decline in business performance;
- an insensitive, abrasive and intimidating style;
- a cold, aloof, arrogant personality;
- betrayed trust;
- over-managing;
- being overly ambitious;
- poor staffing;
- an inability to be strategic;
- an inability to adapt to a boss or culture;
- being over-dependent on an individual's support;
- specific skill deficiencies.

In fact, many of the characteristics of a successful manager can, very easily, become those of a derailed manager. For a manager to avoid this trap, the key is continuous personal development – only by constantly improving and enhancing skills can managers continue to develop.

This also relates to the ability of the high performers to behave as fish in water. While a great many managers refuse to acknowledge or adapt to changing situations, the high performers are adept at changing with the new circumstances. In their daily activities they are continually taking on different persona and different techniques to get their messages across. As criteria for success change, so too must the managers – the alternative is to be left behind.

Table 4.5

Success and high performance	Traditional measurements of success
Continually changing criteria of success.	Rigid view of success.
Progress towards long-term vision.	Achievement of targets.
Creation of long-term vision.	Creation of targets.
Financial; organisational; environmental; personal.	Financial.
Continuous strategy formulation.	Creation of strategy.
Personal development.	Status and career advancement.
Improved effectiveness.	Meeting financial targets.

References

1 Peter Drucker, quoted in David Clutterbuck and Stuart Crainer, *Makers of Management*, Macmillan, 1990.
2 Alan Bowkett, 'Profile', *Independent on Sunday*, 6 June 1993.
3 Economist Intelligence Unit, *On Course for Success*, Economist Intelligence Unit, 1993.
4 Sir John Harvey Jones, *Managing to Survive*, Heinemann, 1992.

5 Frederick Herzberg, quoted in David Clutterbuck and Stuart Crainer, *Makers of Management*, Macmillan, 1990.
6 Chris Argyris, 'Teaching smart people how to learn', *Harvard Business Review*, May/June, 1991.
7 Interview with Patricia Marshall, April 1993.
8 Kevin Barham and Elizabeth Braiden, 'Assessing high potentials', *Directions*, September, 1993.
9 Cooper's and Lybrand, *People's Training and Development*, Cooper's and Lybrand, 1992.
10 Chris Argyris, 'Teaching smart people how to learn', *Harvard Business Review*, May/June 1991.
11 Dr Christina Townsend, 'My biggest mistake', *Independent on Sunday*, 25 July 1993.
12 Pauline Tagg, 'Private face, public face', *Business Life*, October 1993.
13 David Grayson, 'A convergence of values', *Directions*, September 1993.
14 Barbara Clegg, *The Man Who Made Littlewoods*, Hodder & Stoughton, 1993.
15 Richard Pascale, *Managing on the Edge*, Penguin Books, 1991.
16 Nick Faldo, quoted in preview of USPGA championships, *Independent on Sunday*, 8 August 1993.
17 Jerry Cope, 'One to one training: the personal touch', *Business Life*, May 1993.
18 Philip Sadler and Keith Milmer, *The Talent Intensive Organisation*, Economist Intelligence Unit, 1993.
19 Jean-Louis Barsoux, 'Living up to expectations', *The Times*, 20 May 1993.
20 *Journal of General Management*, Vol. 17, No. 4, Summer 1992.
21 Derek Wadlow, 'The odd job man', *The Observer*, 23 May 1993.
22 Philip Sadler and Keith Milmer, *The Talent Intensive Organisation*, Economist Intelligence Unit, 1993
23 Joel Bleeke and David Ernst, *Collaborating to Compete*, John Wiley, 1993.
24 Ramon Pajares, 'Hotel update', *Business Life*, July/August 1993.
25 Lord Rothermere, 'Profile', *Independent on Sunday*, 13 June 1993.
26 Osvaldo Ardilles, 'Instincts that point to success', *The Times*, 2 September 1993.
27 Helen Pitcher, 'Instincts that point to success', *The Times*, 2 September 1993.
28 Robert Drummond, 'Instincts that point to success', *The Times*, 2 September 1993.
29 Robert Sharrock, 'Instincts that point to success', *The Times*, 2 September 1993.
30 Colin Carnall, 'Instincts that point to success', *The Times*, 2 September 1993.
31 John Heider, *The Tao of Leadership*, Wildwood House, 1986.
32 George Davies, *What's Next?*, Mercury, 1989.
33 Tim Hely Hutchinson, 'Go-getter of Grub Street', *Independent on Sunday*, 6 June 1993.
34 Victor Kiam, *Going for it!*, Fontana, 1986.
35 Robert Sharrock, 'When your boss lives to work', *The Times*, 17 June 1993.
36 Jonathan Jeffes, 'When your boss lives to work', *The Times*, 17 June 1993.
37 Robert Kaplan, *Beyond Ambition*, Jossey-Bass, 1991.

38 Tim Scott, 'When your boss lives to work', *The Times*, 17 June 1993.
39 Tom Peters, *Liberation Management*, Macmillan, 1993.
40 Alan Webber, 'What's so new about the new economy?', *Harvard Business Review*, November/December 1992.
41 John Cahill, 'The simple successes of BTR', *Marketing Business*, April 1989.
42 Robert Haas, 'Values make the company', *Harvard Business Review*, September/October 1990.
43 Richard Rumelt, quoted in Phil Hodgson, 'Enhancing strategic thought', unpublished paper, 1991.
44 Robert Evered, quoted in Phil Hodgson, 'Enhancing strategic thought', unpublished paper, 1991.
45 Charles Handy, *The Age of Unreason*, Business Books, 1989.
46 Alvin Toffler, *Powershift*, Bantam Books, 1990.
47 Richard Dawkins, *The Blind Watchmaker*, Longman, 1986.
48 Joel Bleeke and David Ernst, *Collaborating to Compete*, John Wiley, 1993.
49 'The factory as a learning laboratory', *Sloan Management Review*, Vol. 34, No. 1, Fall 1992.
50 Ted Levitt, 'The marketing leviathan', *Marketing Business*, January 1989.
51 Chris Argyris, 'Teaching smart people how to learn', *Harvard Business Review*, May/June 1991.
52 Lord Sterling, quoted in Stuart Crainer, *Zeebrugge: Learning from Disaster*, HFA, 1993.
53 Lord Hanson, quoted in Stuart Crainer, *Zeebrugge: Learning from Disaster*, HFA, 1993.
54 Institute of Management, *Are Career Ladders Disappearing?*, Institute of Management, 1993.
55 Bob Broadbent, 'Bench marking as a planning tool', *Gloves Off*, Summer 1993.
56 Michael Lombardo and Robert Gichinger, *Preventing Derailment*, Center for Creative Leadership, 1989.

5

ACHIEVING HIGH PERFORMANCE

With no magical formula to fall back on how can you achieve high performance?

Searching for resonance

On its front cover, a recently published management book has the formula for success. It is, as you would expect, incomprehensible. Managers may not be so easily amused. There is no formula, yet most managers, at one time or another, feel the need for one.

Fats Waller observed that if you needed to ask what rhythm was then you'd probably never know what it was. Over-endowed with rhythm, it was easy for Waller to poke fun at the rhythm-less unfortunates.

Managers are often tempted into following a similar path. A good manager is a good manager. There is no need for close examination of what makes him or her effective. In some cases, perhaps, this is the case. There are managers who are highly successful without going through ritual and painful examination of why that is so. But, even now, after all the exhaustive analyses of managerial techniques and performance, managers do not appear to be really any more effective than they were twenty years ago or more.

High performance is elusive and sometimes illusionary. Often, it is measured solely in terms of financial performance – public unease with high pay awards for senior executives is perhaps a reflection of growing doubts about quantifying managerial effectiveness by way of profitability. There is, we are beginning to believe, more to management that that.

The trouble is that in uncertain and changing times formulae for success are more attractive than ever before.

Managers demand to know the answers. Uncertainty, however, provides only tentative and temporary solutions.

In this new environment the role of managers has changed fundamentally. The high performers combine and integrate a number of different roles into their day-to-day behaviour. At different times they are contributors, networkers, observers, enthusers, counsellors, coaches, specialists, generalists, and much more. Much of what they actually do can be distilled down to a search for resonance.

If a milk bottle is filled with water and then sung to, it appears to sing back. Managers are looking for the same sort of response from their colleagues, subordinates, superiors, customers and suppliers. They want and need to be in tune.

This sort of resonance was something the high performers managed to achieve repeatedly. They achieved it by:

Adapting to change

As circumstances, situations, environments, organisations and markets change so too must the techniques and attitudes of managers. High performers are adept at altering their behaviour – sometimes with great subtlety – to meet changing needs.

Recognising key simplicities

High performers know their own managerial techniques, their limits and their own personal approaches which clear a way through the organisational minefield. If apparently trivial or simplistic techniques work, they use them.

Harnessing obsession

Recognising the complusive side of managers and management, high performers seek to control obsessiveness and provide direction so the dividing line between healthy obsession (committed and outward-looking) and unhealthy obsession (introverted and blinkered) is not crossed.

Unravelling spaghetti

Intuitively or otherwise, the spaghetti of the past has to be made sense of. Only then can managers avoid making the same mistakes and learn from the past for the future.

Recognising intuition

Accepting the potency and relevance of their own intuitive judgements and hunches, high performers use them while not relying on them.

Building on weakness

Weakness is strength. By acknowledging their own limitations and deficiencies, high performers undermine the still common perception that managers are super heroes. Also, recognition opens the way to improvement.

Maintaining realism

High performers are not seduced by the apparent power of their position. They recognise that if management is now a team game, no one member of the team is indispensable.

Going with the pace

Change is not always a sprint, although it often feels as though it is. The pace of change is governed by the size and culture of the organisation. Too much too soon can result in disaster. High performers are able to assess the necessary pace of change and learning so that they can press the accelerator or brake when appropriate.

Accepting the muddle

Clarity of purpose or action cannot always be achieved. In fact, more often than not clarity is soon questioned and complicated by events. High performers accept the muddle but, at the same time, seek to communicate as much clarity as possible.

Using vision

The only static vision is history. The rest we adapt and shape as we go along. Instead of being an inert wall-covering, vision is a day-to-day coda for all activities.

Learning continually

High performers regard learning as a practical necessity rather than an indulgence. They identify learning opportunities on a daily basis and are aware of how they can best learn from them.

Managing uncertainty

In an uncertain world, certainty is a necessary oasis. While being able to live with and thrive on ambiguity, managers need to add certainty to the roles and situations of those they manage.

Balancing short-term and long-term aims

Keeping your eyes on the present, you ignore the future. Managers continually need to keep both in their sights and accept short-term setbacks if they lead a step nearer long-term goals.

Accepting no formula

The lack of easy answers, does not mean that you have to stop looking for solutions. High performers accept that solutions have a short lifespan and today's answers quickly become tomorrow's questions.

Making time to think

Apparently hemmed in by the sheer volume of work, high performers find the time to think. They realise that sound decision-making is not solely based on sound figures, but also on clarifying the issues in their own minds before action is taken.

Making time for colleagues

Although office doors are often open, the minds of managers may not be. High performers open their doors and make time for their colleagues and subordinates consistently so that colleagues and subordinates feel comfortable in confiding and informing.

Making time for customers

Open diaries and flexibility leave the way open for customers to work in partnership.

Channelling energy

Directors rather than dictators; enablers rather than controllers. Managers need now to channel people's energy and commitment in constantly changing directions rather than relying on one hefty push down a straight route to success.

Using the organisation

High performers utilise the resources of their organisation while eschewing pointless political machinations.

Abusing the organisation

No organisation or system is sacred. Assumptions require questioning and systems require pushing to their limits so they can be continually re-defined.

Listening to others

If managers don't listen to others, soon the only voice heard will be their own. Opinions, information, data and spontaneous ideas are willingly listened to and taken on-board by high performers as a ready source of knowledge.

Using language

The jargon of management can render important messages meaningless. Direct and clear use of language is a key means of achieving change and constantly refreshing the management process.

Creating space

If managers fail to define their own space who will do it for them? Setting parameters to their jobs and tasks enables high performers to have a clear idea of what they expect of themselves, their colleagues and organisational resources.

Telling the truth

The truth is as things are. Knowing that, you can move on and achieve change. High performers do not accept organisational truths without rigorous questioning. Having established the real situation, they are blunt in their honesty about what needs to be done and who needs to do it.

Leading by supporting

The leader is one of many contributors. In the era of team work, the more senior the manager the better a team player he or she must be.

Measuring achievement

'Busy-ness' measures inefficiency; achievement is the measure of efficiency. Instead, of measuring effectiveness in terms of numbers of hours worked, managers must seek out new measurements and accept that often their contribution is unquantifiable.

Making decisions obvious

High performers seek to make strategies and decisions as obviously logical and clear-cut as possible. They do not railroad them through, but make their rightfulness unassailable.

Using travel

Instead of accepting travel as an occupational hazard, high performers utilise the opportunity to talk to colleagues and use their time effectively. In addition, they use the modern ease of international travel to become closer to geographically distant units and managers.

INDEX